10 Steps to Mastering Stress

10 Steps to Mastering Stress

A LIFESTYLE APPROACH

Updated Edition

David H. Barlow, PhD

Ronald M. Rapee, PhD

Sarah Perini, MA

OXFORD
UNIVERSITY PRESS

OXFORD

UNIVERSITY PRESS

Oxford University Press is a department of the University of
Oxford. It furthers the University's objective of excellence in research,
scholarship, and education by publishing worldwide.

Oxford   New York

Auckland   Cape Town   Dar es Salaam   Hong Kong   Karachi
Kuala Lumpur   Madrid   Melbourne   Mexico City   Nairobi
New Delhi   Shanghai   Taipei   Toronto

With offices in

Argentina   Austria   Brazil   Chile   Czech Republic   France   Greece
Guatemala   Hungary   Italy   Japan   Poland   Portugal   Singapore
South Korea   Switzerland   Thailand   Turkey   Ukraine   Vietnam

Oxford is a registered trademark of Oxford University Press
in the UK and certain other countries.

Published in the United States of America by
Oxford University Press
198 Madison Avenue, New York, NY 10016

Library of Congress Cataloging-in-Publication Data
Barlow, David H.
10 steps to mastering stress: a lifestyle approach / David H. Barlow, Ph.D.,
Ronald M. Rapee, Ph.D. Sarah Perini, M.A.—Updated edition.
pages cm
ISBN 978–0–19–991753–2
1. Stress (Psychology)   2. Stress management.   I. Rapee, Ronald M.
II. Perini, Sarah.   III. Title.   IV. Title: Ten steps to mastering stress.
BF575.S75B2958 2014
155.9'042—dc23
2013028791

3 5 7 9 8 6 4 2
Printed in the United States of America
on acid-free paper

CONTENTS

INTRODUCTION

From the outside, Joe looked like a classic success story. At age 45, he owned a profitable business, had a beautiful family, and had just built a new home. Inside, however, Joe felt miserable. Although he stayed at work later and later each night, he never seemed to accomplish enough. When he finally arrived home, his head was pounding, and he yelled at his children so often that they began to shy away from him. Nothing made Joe happy—not his business, not his family, and, most of all, not himself. Each day brought new irritations, until one day Joe looked around and realized that he was hurting everything and everyone that mattered to him.

Stress was ruining Joe's life. He is not alone. Stress is a common problem facing people in today's complex world. You can't see it, hear it, or smell it, yet stress can threaten both your physical health and psychological well-being.

If you are a chronic worrier, if you push yourself toward perfection each day and then punish yourself for all that you have not accomplished, then you are waging your own battle with stress. Perhaps you are irritable and tense most of the time, and your doctor has said that stress is causing your headaches and upset stomach.

Different people react to stress in different ways. Whatever your own response may be, it is important to know one thing: You can learn to master stress and the problems it causes you. Our 10-step program will help you identify what is causing your stress, teach you to relax, and show you how to think more realistically. It will also give you strategies for dealing with the stressful events life can throw at you. You will emerge calmer and more in control. Picking up this book was your first move toward these goals.

The program presented in this book is the result of over three decades of research, first at the Center for Stress and Anxiety Disorders at the State University of New York at Albany and, more recently, at the Center for Anxiety and Related Disorders, Boston University. This is the largest research center of its kind in the world, and, in recent years, researchers at the center have learned more about stress than was ever known before. In Australia, we have continued this research in the Centre for Emotional Health at Macquarie University. Hundreds of people who have come to these clinics for help have followed a program like this one and found themselves much better able to cope with stress.

We have selected four case studies that we will follow throughout the book as they apply each of the 10 steps. These case studies are based on combinations of actual patients we have seen in our clinics. You will see that they have a range of backgrounds and life circumstances, and experience their stress in different ways. Perhaps you will relate to one or more of them. We hope that their examples will illustrate how you can apply our 10 steps to reduce stress in your own life.

WHY MASTER STRESS?

In recent years, we have come to realize just how important controlling stress can be for our well-being. It has become clear that stress can interfere with many parts of our lives—stress increases the chance of developing diseases, it increases work absenteeism, it can lead to relationship difficulties and interpersonal strain, and it can increase the risk of turning to artificial relaxation such as drugs and alcohol. On the extreme side, stress increases the risk of developing serious illnesses in the future, and even on the mild side, stress can reduce our enjoyment of life. Stress claims from workers' compensation have been on the rise. Stress costs the community vast amounts of money each year—both from direct medical and legal claims and from indirect costs associated with missed work, divorce, and accidents. So, as you can see, reducing your stress will be of tremendous benefit, not only to you personally, but also to the community as a whole.

WHO IS THIS BOOK FOR?

This book is for people who would like to use effective, research-based techniques to reduce their levels of stress or anxiety. The 10 steps outlined in this book are based on years of psychological research at leading universities. This research has tested the techniques with many people, ranging from those with ordinary, day-to-day stress through to those whose stress is so overwhelming that it is interfering with their ability to relate to their families and friends, accomplish what they need to at work, or generally enjoy life. Regardless of whether your stress is occasional or ongoing, you will likely benefit from implementing the techniques in this book.

This book is NOT for you if:

- You are looking for a "quick fix" solution to your stress that doesn't involve any effort on your part. Simply reading the book will not be effective. For the techniques to work, they must be practiced regularly.
- You are currently experiencing clinical depression. Clinical depression is different from the temporary feelings of sadness, flatness, or grief that most people experience from time to time. Clinical depression is a mood disorder that involves persistent feelings of sadness or flatness for most of the day, nearly every day, for a period of two weeks or more. People

who are clinically depressed also experience a range of other persistent symptoms, such as ongoing problems with sleep and appetite, disinterest in things they used to enjoy, and feelings of worthlessness. If this sounds like you, we recommend that you seek assistance from your family doctor, psychologist, or psychiatrist without delay. With professional treatment, it is likely that your mood will improve. You will then be in a much better position to work through this book.

HOW IS THIS PROGRAM DIFFERENT?

While there are many books on stress on the market, this program differs from most for some important reasons.

As described above, this program has been scientifically developed and tested to ensure that it is the most effective way to master stress. While many other books are based simply on the authors' ideas and opinions, the elements of this program have been extensively tested. In order to test this extensively, hundreds of stressed individuals have completed the program and have been compared with stressed people who were not on the program to objectively demonstrate its effectiveness.

Rather than simply listing various techniques in a random manner, this book describes a systematic program that sets out how to learn and integrate the relevant techniques into your life in a step-by-step fashion. We also follow four case studies so that, for every step, you get clear illustrations of how the techniques are applied. The record forms we provide will help you to apply the techniques in your own life. These can be photocopied or downloaded from the following website: www.oup.com/us/ttw.

The techniques we describe are common-sense procedures that work when they are applied in a consistent and systematic manner to the problems in your life. We don't sell these techniques as "cure-alls" but emphasize the importance of regular practice. Most important, we don't try to claim that the program described in this book will magically lift away your stress. Rather, we reinforce the importance of making these techniques a part of your daily life—a lifestyle approach.

ARE YOU READY?

The only person who can change your stress level is you. Our program can help, but the motivation and the time must come from you. If you work hard, you will be rewarded. People who have completed this program report that they are enjoying life more and that their friends and family enjoy them more.

In the chapters that follow, you will be learning new skills—new ways of thinking, acting, and organizing your life. The key term you will hear over and over is *practice*. If you practice these skills, and practice hard, we are confident you will learn to master your stress.

The goal is not to eliminate all stress but rather to reduce your stress to a manageable level. None of us can live without a little stress in our lives.

If you have been troubled by stress for a long time, a doctor may have prescribed a tranquilizer or other medication for you. It is perfectly acceptable to continue taking those medications while working through the lessons in this program. If you wish to stop your regularly prescribed medication during or after this program, we recommend that you consult your doctor.

It is also important to recognize that life is full of unfortunate happenings—divorce, illness, death of loved ones—all of which can cause stress. Obviously, this program cannot cancel a divorce or bring someone you loved back to life. What it will do is help you deal with your reactions to these situations, so that stress does not control your life. The techniques you will learn in this program can also help you find a more direct solution to other types of problems, such as the small, everyday hassles and burdens we all encounter.

SET YOUR GOALS

It is never easy to find the motivation to accomplish a difficult task, and it is even harder to keep motivated when the rewards are weeks or months away. So before you get started, try these three simple exercises to ease your way into the program:

1. *Think about why you want to change.*

What is stress doing to the quality of your life? On the chart below, make a list of all the negative effects you can see stress causing. Maybe you lie awake at night worrying about everything you have to do, bicker with your spouse, or make careless errors at work. Examine your life honestly, and write down the negatives caused by stress.

2. *Think about how your life will be better once you have mastered stress.*

Maybe you will have fewer headaches or less trouble with that nervous stomach. Maybe you will be able to enjoy sitting down and relaxing with friends without worrying about how much you have to do. Also on the chart below, list the positives you aim for in the future. Make a copy of your list and place it in a prominent place, perhaps on the refrigerator or near your bed. When the going gets tough, look at it and think of the positive benefits you are working toward.

Negative Effects in My Life Caused by Stress	Positive Effects in My Life When I've Mastered My Stress

3. Devote time to this program.

If you are serious about reducing your stress, you will need to devote plenty of time to this program. You need to read each step, often more than once to really understand it, and you need to practice the exercises many times. It is a good idea to set aside a time each week when you will read over the next step or review where you are and plan your coming week. There is no "set" speed, but mostly you could aim to move to the next step each week. On some steps you may feel you need more practice, and you could stay with a step for two or even three weeks. If you are working through this program with a therapist, your weekly therapy time will serve as the weekly review. So, overall, the whole program should take you around 12 to 15 weeks.

MEET OUR CASE STUDIES

We have selected the following case studies to illustrate the way this program can be applied to real people with real stress. For every technique we introduce, we will draw on these case studies to show how they can be practically applied.

Anne

Anne is 57. She works full time as a bookkeeper, and she is married with one daughter. Anne's husband recently lost his job, and he is finding it difficult to find other work. Their 32-year-old daughter, Ellie, has recently moved back home after splitting up with her partner. Anne feels worried about both her daughter and her husband. She wants to assist them both as much as she can, but she also resents the fact that she is doing most of the housework, as well as working full time. Anne finds herself snapping at her family, and then feels guilty. She isn't sleeping well and is often tired.

Erik

Erik is 31. He is employed full time as a draftsman and is also trying to complete an architecture degree. He started the degree several years ago but has found it difficult to complete assignments on time. Consequently, the degree is taking much longer than he anticipated, and he feels desperate to finish it. However, there never seems to be enough time in the day. Erik always has a long "to-do" list in his head and can't seem to switch off. He has gained a lot of weight in the past few years, and his doctor is urging him to lose it. But Erik doesn't have time to exercise or cook and feels completely overwhelmed by the demands of his life. Over the past few months Erik's mood has really taken a nosedive. He feels as though nothing much is fun anymore and wonders if things will ever get better.

Rhani

Rhani is 22. She lives with two friends and works full time in a beauty salon. Rhani's boss is quite critical and demanding, and Rhani finds her hard to work with. Rhani feels so stressed by the situation that she often feels very sick before work in the morning and finds it hard to feel happy, even on her days off. Rhani has always been quite a shy person, and she hates conflict. She worries a lot about what other people think of her and is finding her work situation to be almost unbearable.

Joe

Joe is 45. He owns a real estate agency and is married, with two sons at school. Joe's friends tell him that he should be happy, as he has a lovely family, successful business, and a brand-new house. However, he doesn't feel happy at all. Joe has high standards and is constantly disappointed by his own, and others', failure to meet them. He finds himself frequently losing his temper with his staff and his family. Joe's wife often begs him to "chill out" and relax, but he honestly doesn't know how this is possible.

Keep reading to find out how Anne, Erik, Rhani, and Joe implemented our 10-step program to reduce their stress and lead happier, more relaxed lives.

10 Steps to Mastering Stress

Understand Your Stress

THE BASICS OF STRESS

Simply put, stress is a state of readiness. It is the mind's and the body's way of rising to an occasion and preparing you to do your best. Although the effects of too much stress can be debilitating, stress itself is a completely natural and necessary response, one experienced by all humans and animals.

Stress is not—repeat, not—a mental illness. Just as people's heights vary over a wide range from short to tall, people's everyday stress levels vary over a wide range from relaxed to "stressed out." Stress, no matter how extreme, will never make you "go crazy."

Stress is a natural occurrence and has a very useful function. Let's say, for example, that you were going to be a contestant on a television quiz show. If you felt no stress at all, you may not prepare for the show, and as a result might do poorly. If, however, you felt extremely stressed, you may be too nervous to study and could become confused and distracted when the cameras started rolling. But if you felt a mild amount of stress, you would prepare well in advance, concentrate better, and react faster when the questions were asked. The physical and mental responses that constitute stress are useful if they happen occasionally and in moderation. But if they happen all the time, day in and day out, they can have unpleasant effects.

Experiencing a high level of stress for a long time can cause you to lose sleep, feel constantly fatigued, have trouble concentrating, and respond irritably to those around you. Long-term stress can also cause headaches, skin irritations, ulcers, diarrhea, and pains at the base of the jaw (temporomandibular joint [TMJ] syndrome). Stress can interfere with sexual function, inhibiting both desire and ability. Research also shows that long-term stress may increase your chances of later developing heart disease, high blood pressure, diabetes, or immune system problems.

Although this list may look intimidating, you should not add to your stress by worrying about health problems. Being highly stressed does not mean that you will get diseases, merely that you may increase your susceptibility over time. Clearly, reducing stress can have important benefits, both mentally and physically.

WHY AM I STRESSED?

If you are reading this book, you may be wondering why other people do not seem to be as stressed as you. Stress is not a disease, nor a sign of weakness. Feelings of stress come from a combination of two different sources: the world around you and your way of dealing with that world. These two sources, the environment and your personality, interact to produce your actual levels of stress. Sometimes your life can be filled with so many stressful events that it is no wonder you feel overwhelmed. But stressful events are not enough. We all know of people who don't seem to become flustered no matter how difficult the situation. These "cool customers" seem to have personalities that can deal with any situation, no matter how tough. On the other hand, there are some people who seem to make "mountains out of molehills" no matter what the situation. For these people, no matter how small the event, it still seems that they will make themselves stressed.

But personality is not the whole story. Different situations vary in how stress provoking they are. The more difficult the situation, the more people you will find who become stressed and the more stressed these people become. So you can see that in any situation, the degree of stress you will feel depends on a combination of the type of event happening at the time (how stress provoking it is) and the way you respond to or deal with that event (your personality). Therefore, to change your stress levels, you can either change the world around you or change the way you respond to that world, or both. Surprisingly, it is often easier to change your own responses than to change what goes on around you. However, it is also quite often possible to do the latter.

In this program we will be teaching you to consider both parts of the stress response. In the first part of the program (Steps 2 through 5) we will teach you different ways of coping with the world around you—for example, modifying your personality. In the second part of the program (Steps 6 through 8), we will talk about ways in which you might actually change your environment to make it less challenging. Let's discuss these sources of stress in more detail.

STRESSFUL ENVIRONMENTS

We all know that there are lots of things in our world that can make us stressed. Usually we think of the big things—losing a job, death of a partner, a serious car accident, or approaching deadlines. True, these are all events that, when they occur, can make us very stressed. But we also need to remember what scientists call "daily hassles." These are many of life's more general, smaller events that are annoying, irritating, and unpleasant and can be an ongoing source of stress. Some examples of daily hassles might be heavy traffic on the way to work, an unpleasant work colleague, noise around the home, or an overdependent relative. In fact, because they are so common and tend to add up, daily hassles are often more of a problem for most of us than major life events. It is important also to remember that positive things can sometimes be stressful because of the negative aspects that go with them. For example, going on a vacation can actually be a major source of stress because of the organization and extra work you have to do to get away. Finally, the circumstances of our lives can be constant and ongoing sources of stress. Some of these are things we can't do much about, such as being poor, having an abusive parent, or living in a high-crime area. Others have a lot to do with our choices in life, such as trying to raise three children and have two jobs, working for a company that demands too much, or struggling to pay off that expensive vacation that you really couldn't afford.

HANDLING OUR ENVIRONMENT

The way we cope with stressful events like those described above is really a part of our personalities. As with any personality characteristic, your general stress level has two major components: genetics and environment. Researchers are still trying to pinpoint the exact genetic component to stress. What is most likely is that there is no specific stress gene. Rather, if you are a highly stressed person, you may have inherited a tendency to be generally emotional. In other words, you may find that you are more sensitive and generally emotional than many other people you know. On the negative side, this means that you will respond to challenges with higher levels of stress. But on the bright side, this tendency probably makes you a sensitive and caring individual. The genetic factor, of course, only means that you may be predisposed to feeling stressed—it does not mean that stress is inevitable. Even if you have a genetic predisposition to stress, you can learn to manage it.

Much of your personality probably comes from your environment, from things that you have learned over the course of your life. These things may have been learned from your parents or from the circumstances and experiences of your life. These lessons vary from person to person, and we can't necessarily describe them here. But we do know that people who feel high stress in a lot of situations tend to have two major beliefs:

1. They believe that their world is full of negatives.
2. They believe that they don't have as much control as they would like over the negatives in their lives.

If you can identify with these beliefs, just remember that it took you a long time to learn them. You are not going to unlearn them overnight. But with hard work and practice, your outlook can change. We will not be looking into your past to try and determine what caused your original tendency toward stress. You will not be expected to regress back to your childhood or to blame your parents. Instead, you will be learning practical skills to help you control stress here and now. If you cannot identify with these issues at this point, don't worry. We will discuss them in more detail in a later chapter, and we hope that you will find that they begin to make more sense.

FACING CHALLENGES

When you perceive a potential threat or challenge, your mind and body prepare you to deal with it. The danger does not have to be real; anything you perceive as a threat or challenge triggers your body and mind to get ready. Actual physical threats are not the only trigger. Potential failure or ridicule is a major source of stress for most people.

Let's consider an example. Imagine that you are walking home at night and your route takes you down a deserted lane. As soon as you enter the lane, you are on alert. Your mind and body are preparing themselves to take action in the event you are confronted with danger. Though it may not be immediately apparent, the purpose of stress is to protect you. If a mugger suddenly jumped from the shadows in the lane, you would be physically ready to respond quickly.

The challenge of deadlines provides another common example. When you have an important report due in an hour and you haven't finished it yet, you feel stress, in this case because of the potential failure that is involved if you don't finish the report. When your sister is coming to pick you up in a few minutes and your children are screaming and you haven't had time to take a shower, you feel stress.

In both of these cases, the threat is not the deadline itself. It is the fear that you will fail and that someone important to you, your boss or your sister, will criticize you for letting them down. If you cared nothing about these people, you would not have these stressful feelings. But most of us do care; therefore, most of us would feel stress in similar situations. This shows how the environment (approaching deadline) interacts with your personality (caring about your boss's opinions) to produce your level of stress. The closer the deadline, the higher your stress. In the same way, the more you care about your boss's opinion, the higher your stress. Your final level of stress, then, will depend on a combination of the environment and your personality.

THE STRESS RESPONSE SYSTEMS

Stress is a response to some sort of potential negative that we perceive in our environment. The word "stress" is a broad, poorly defined term that we use to refer to a large range of responses to negatives. When you perceive a situation as having some potential negatives, you attempt to deal with that situation and eliminate the negative. If you do this successfully, you feel positive emotions. But if the situation is beyond your ability to cope, you experience a range of negative reactions that are broadly labeled "stress." The various emotions you might experience include anger, anxiety, and depression. When you experience these feelings, your mind and body will react in certain ways. These are described below.

The Physical System

The physical or physiological response system includes all the changes that take place in your body when you are stressed. Some of these changes can seem quite bizarre and frightening when they are unfamiliar. But rest assured that they are all natural, important, and, in the short term, harmless. However, if stress is maintained for long periods, your body's immune system can begin to break down, leaving you more susceptible to developing diseases.

When you perceive or anticipate a threat, your brain sends messages to a section of your nerves called the autonomic nervous system. This system has two branches, the *sympathetic* and *parasympathetic* nervous systems. Simply stated, the sympathetic nervous system releases energy and gets the body primed for action. Later, the parasympathetic nervous system returns the body to a normal state.

The sympathetic nervous system releases two chemicals, *adrenalin* and *noradrenalin*, from the adrenal glands on the kidneys. Fueled by these two chemicals, the activity of the sympathetic nervous system can continue for some time.

Activity in the sympathetic nervous system makes your heart beat more rapidly and your blood flow much faster and differently. By tightening your blood vessels, your sympathetic nervous system directs blood away from places where it is not needed, such as skin, fingers, and toes, and moves it toward places where it is needed more, such as your arm and leg muscles. For this reason, when you experience extreme stress, your skin may look pale and your fingers and toes tingle or become numb. Meanwhile, the value of this effect for your survival is that the blood flow has primed your large muscles for action.

The rapid heart rate and fast breathing you experience when under stress help to provide more oxygen to your body. Although this is important for fast action, the change can make you feel as if you are choking or smothering, and may cause chest pains. In addition, the reduced blood supply to your head can make you feel dizzy or confused, causing blurred vision or a feeling of unreality.

Overall, stress affects most of the systems in your body. This process takes a lot of energy, which explains why you feel drained at the end of a stressful day. It is important to know, however, that your sympathetic nervous system cannot get "carried away" and leave you in a state of "high stress" indefinitely. Your body has two safeguards to prevent this. First, other chemicals in the body will eventually destroy the adrenalin and noradrenalin released by the sympathetic nervous system. Second, the parasympathetic nervous system is a built-in protector. When your body has "had enough" of the stress response, the parasympathetic nervous system will kick in to restore a relaxed feeling. This may not happen as quickly as you would like, but it will happen. Your body will not allow your stress to keep increasing until you "explode."

In addition to the effects on your autonomic nervous system, feeling stressed produces a release of chemicals from your pituitary gland (a small area at the base of the skull). These chemicals travel to another section of your adrenal gland to release various corticoids and steroids that help to reduce swelling and inflammation. If stress is prolonged, the constant release of these chemicals can also produce some damage to your body (e.g., in the circulatory system) and make you more susceptible to disease.

The physical responses that prepare you for action, as well as those involved in calming you down, are largely automatic. You cannot eliminate them altogether, nor would you want to. As we have said before, stress serves an important protective function. It can lead to greater accomplishment and even, under the right circumstances, be enjoyable. In the short term, stress is not harmful, and small amounts of stress can actually have some benefits. But if you experience high levels of stress for long periods of your life, you may be more likely to have physical problems. Obviously, learning to control your stress is important for many reasons.

The Mental System

Your body is not alone in preparing for action when you face a challenge or threat. Your mind also gets into the act. The major mental, or *cognitive*, response is to change your focus of attention. When you are under stress, you tend to scan the environment constantly, looking for signs of threat. On one hand, this shift in attention is useful; if danger exists, you will notice it quickly. On the other hand, you may feel easily distracted and unable to concentrate on any one thing.

As part of this scanning process, your mind considers all the possible outcomes of a threatening situation. In other words, you have a lot of anxious thoughts or, as most of us would put it, you worry. Worrying is one of the main characteristics of people under stress. A little worrying is normal; everyone does it. Many of us worry about the same kinds of things. But people who are continually stressed have trouble turning off the worrying. Sometimes they even feel they need to worry, fearing the lack of worrying might be irresponsible. Try to avoid falling into this trap! Being responsible is an admirable goal. But if you have reached the point where the thoughts churning through your head are keeping you awake at night, worrying is not helping you. In fact, it's hurting you. We will be teaching you ways of controlling your worry later in this program.

Let's apply these components of the mental response to our example of walking through a dark lane. As you walked, you would literally be scanning, looking and listening for possible danger. If there were a sudden noise, even from a harmless stray cat, you would most likely jump. But if a mugger appeared, you would probably spot him quickly. The worrying in this case might take the form of questions running through your mind: "Is he going to hurt me?" "Does he have friends around?" "Does he have a gun?" To some extent, this worrying is useful; it prepares you for the possibilities.

In the example of the late report, you would probably concentrate hard on the task at hand. In this situation, your focus would not be on scanning, but chances are you would still be worrying, asking yourself: "What if I don't finish on time?" "What will my boss say?" "What would I do if I lost this job?" These worries may be useful if they remind you of how important the task is. But if the worries become so great that they interfere with your ability to finish the report, you may have started a vicious cycle. Worrying could make you miss the deadline, which would cause you to lose confidence in yourself. Without confidence, you may miss the next deadline, and then you would feel even more stressed than you did before. Obviously, you do not want to let worrying go this far.

The Behavioral System

Stress is also likely to influence some of the ways you behave. You may act irritably, or you may start to avoid situations that you fear could be stressful. In fact, to return to our first example, you would probably avoid the lane entirely if you thought it looked dangerous—in which case stress and the anticipation of danger would actually have protected you. On the other hand, in our deadline example, avoiding the report (or procrastinating) shows how stress can really interfere with tasks.

Many people get jittery when they are under stress. You are probably familiar with your own nervous habits: pacing, tapping your feet, biting your nails, smoking, or snacking. Whatever your habit is, you will probably notice yourself doing more of it when you are under stress. Most of these behaviors are simply ways of letting off some of the energy that has built up from your physical and mental preparation for action. Still others (such as escaping from or avoiding unpleasant situations) are there to protect you. The rest may be individually learned ways of trying to calm down.

As with the other response systems, these behaviors are generally harmless and may even be beneficial when realized in moderation. But they can become excessive and begin to interfere with your enjoyment of life. Importantly, when avoidance becomes severe it can make you miss important opportunities, which can lead to even more stress.

THE STRESS RESPONSE SPIRAL

The physical, mental, and behavioral response systems each have their own purposes. But they also interact closely. Any one system can trigger the whole spiral. For example, you may notice your heart beginning to pound. This, in turn, could trigger thoughts that something is wrong. You begin to pace nervously back and forth. Alternately, you may begin with a worrisome thought about the children that may cause your body to react and then make you want to rush home to check on them. Because each system plays a role in the entire stress response, it is important to learn to control each one. This is what our stress management program will help you do.

At the physical level, you will learn to recognize tension in your body before it becomes excessive, and you will learn strategies to help you relax. To address the mental component of stress, we will teach you more realistic ways of thinking about situations so that they do not seem as threatening. Finally, at the behavioral level, you will practice new ways of responding to situations. You will learn through experience that threats may not be threats at all, or they may not be as bad as you fear. Using these techniques will help to teach you new ways of coping with your environment. In addition, at various points in the program, we will describe ways in which you might try and actually change your environment to make it less stress provoking for you.

YOUR OWN STRESS

Now that you understand the way that stress operates in general, it is time to find out more about your own personal experience of stress. What situations lead to stress for you? How does stress affect your body? What goes through your mind when you are stressed? And how do you behave?

You may feel that you can answer some of these questions easily. Or you may not know the answers at this stage. Either way, the first step of managing stress is to understand your own personal triggers and reactions better. The best way to do this is to keep records. Records are important for several reasons:

1. Identifying triggers

The things that cause stress are known as "triggers," and they are different for each of us. Some of them are large, life-changing events like those noted below. Others are everyday occurrences, minor hassles that might not bother others but that are legitimately stressful for you.

When you do not know what is causing your stress, the responses of your mind and body can seem frightening and unexplainable. Keeping records will help you to identify your stress triggers, thus giving you a greater sense of control.

Triggers that may cause stress include:

- Getting married
- Work deadlines
- Death of close friend or relative
- Having a baby
- Changes in work roles
- Break-up of a relationship
- Financial pressures
- Home repairs
- School examinations
- Car maintenance
- Changing jobs
- Legal matters
- Car accident
- Job interview

2. Gaining objectivity

None of us know all there is to know about our own physical and emotional responses. For example, you may think that on any given day, you are either stressed or not, all or nothing. In fact, you probably experience many degrees of stress.

Keeping records will help you to identify the various ways that you react to stressful situations. You may also begin to realize that more of your physical responses are connected to stress than you might have thought. Keeping records of these responses helps make the whole process more understandable.

3. Staying motivated

If you keep honest records, you are more likely to practice each technique as recommended. You will also be able to give yourself credit for what you have accomplished.

4. Learning skills

Writing out the details in a structured way helps you to understand how each technique works and how it affects you.

The three forms that follow—the **Daily Stress Record**, **Stressful Events Record**, and the **Progress Chart**—will help you to understand your own stress. We recommend that you complete these for the next two to three weeks, or longer if possible.

DAILY STRESS RECORD

The first form is the Daily Stress Record. You may wish to prepare your own version of the form, or take the one we have provided and print it. Then, every evening, sit down with the form and think back over your day. How stressful was it? You will be recording three things in particular:

1. Your average level of stress during the day

The average level means the overall, background level of stress you felt during the day as a whole. Was it a "good day" during which you felt fairly relaxed most of the time? Was it a "bad day" during which you were constantly tense? Or did the day fall somewhere in between?

You will notice that we ask you to keep this record using a scale from 0 to 8, where 0 is no stress and 8 is extreme stress. We will be using this 0–8 scale at many points throughout the program. It is important that you grow familiar with it and practice assigning your responses to some point along the scale.

$$0 \longrightarrow 1 \longrightarrow 2 \longrightarrow 3 \longrightarrow 4 \longrightarrow 5 \longrightarrow 6 \longrightarrow 7 \longrightarrow 8$$

NONE   MILD   MODERATE   MUCH   EXTREME

2. The highest level of stress you experienced during the day

If nothing significant happened during the day and you did not become more stressed than your average level, the numbers in the first two columns will be the same. It is likely, however, that your stress level increased in response to at least a few things, small or large, that happened. Using the 0–8 scale, write down the number that best corresponds to your highest stress level of the day.

3. Any major stressful events that happened during the day

This is the place to list the event or events responsible for the highest level you listed in column two. This final column serves an important explanatory purpose. Say, for example, that you recorded your average stress level as 2 on Monday, but it rose to 5 on Tuesday. If you experienced a sudden rush of orders at work Tuesday, or left work to find your car broken into, the increase is understandable. Unless you note the reasons on the form, however, you may not remember later what caused your stress.

The Daily Stress Record has an important purpose. It helps you to gauge your feelings more realistically. When it comes to stress, your mind can play tricks on you. For example, how often have you said on Friday, "Boy, this was a terrible week"? Looking back at your stress records, however, you may discover that in reality only one day went badly. In this way, record keeping can contribute to your peace of mind. Here are sample Daily Stress Records, taken from each of our case studies:

Daily Stress Record—Anne

Date	Average Stress	Highest Stress	Stressful Events
6/5	4	5	Opened electricity bill.
6/6	4	6	Car wouldn't start.
6/7	5	6	Couldn't sleep.

Daily Stress Record—Erik

Date	Average Stress	Highest Stress	Stressful Events
10/26	5	7	Studying for test. Assignment is overdue.
10/27	5	6	Angry e-mail from a client.
10/28	4	5	Weighed self.

Daily Stress Record—Rhani

Date	Average Stress	Highest Stress	Stressful Events
4/12	5	6	Dinner with Matt's friends.
4/13	6	7	Forgot how to process a refund at work. Boss rolled eyes and sighed.
4/14	2	3	Slept in and had to rush.

Daily Stress Record—Joe

Date	Average Stress	Highest Stress	Stressful Events
8/9	4	6	Argument with Mel.
8/10	5	6	Mike wrote terrible report, and I had to redo it.
8/11	5	7	Traffic!!

STRESSFUL EVENTS RECORD

Although you can leave the Daily Stress Record at home and fill it out at night, you should carry the Stressful Events Record with you, so that you can fill it out whenever you notice yourself feeling stressed. That may sound like a burden, but do not worry. You will need to use this form for only a few weeks. Its purpose is to show you more about how you react to certain events. In our experience, many of the clients that we see have a limited understanding of their own responses—they don't know exactly how they respond to stress. The Stressful Events Record will help you understand your own responses better.

Use the Stressful Events Record every time your stress level rises. Some days you may record many episodes of stress, while other days you may record none. You will find a blank form on page 17 that you may photocopy. Alternatively, you can download it from our website: www.oup.com/us/ttw. The following instructions will help you complete the Stressful Events Record.

- Note the approximate time that your stress began to increase.
- Note the approximate time that the level returned to normal.
- Use the 0–8 scale to note the highest level of stress you felt during this particular episode.
- If you know what triggered the stress, note the event or events. This column is likely to echo the "major stressful events" column on your Daily Stress Record for that day.
- Record the major physical symptoms you experienced as a result of this stress—headaches, nausea, pounding heart, or other symptoms.
- Finally, write down the thoughts that went through your head as your stress was increasing. For example, you may have thought, "I won't make it, I can't cope" or "I'm going to look foolish." No matter how silly the thoughts seem after the moment has passed, write them down.

Filling out the Stressful Events Record will help you identify your own particular stress triggers and responses. After a time, you may notice a pattern to your stress, which could point to a specific problem for you to address. Sample Stressful Events Records from our case studies are shown here.

Stressful Events Record—Anne

Date	Starting Time	Ending Time	Highest Stress (0–8)	Triggers	Symptoms	Thoughts
6/7	10 p.m.	11:30 p.m.	6	Trying to get to sleep.	Restless, hot.	I can't sleep. I need to sleep well because I have so much to do tomorrow. I won't cope if I'm tired.

Stressful Events Record—Erik

Date	Starting Time	Ending Time	Highest Stress (0–8)	Triggers	Symptoms	Thoughts
10/26	8 a.m.	11 p.m.	7	Studying plus have assignment overdue.	Agitated, fidgety. Can't concentrate. Back is aching.	I'll never get all this done. I should drop out of this course.

Stressful Events Record—Rhani

Date	Starting Time	Ending Time	Highest Stress (0–8)	Triggers	Symptoms	Thoughts
4/12	4 p.m.	8 p.m.	7	Dinner with Matt's friends.	Palms sweating, knots in stomach.	I'll have nothing to say. They'll think I'm boring.

Stressful Events Record—Joe

Date	Starting Time	Ending Time	Highest Stress (0–8)	Triggers	Symptoms	Thoughts
8/10	11 a.m.	1 p.m.	6	Mike gave me his report to review.	Clenching my jaw and fists.	This is hopeless! I'll need to do it again and I don't have time. He's an idiot.

PROGRESS CHART

As you follow this stress management program, you will want to keep track of your progress. Over the weeks, you should notice a gradual drop in your level of stress. Again, however, your mind can play tricks on you. Because you may not remember how you felt before the program, you may not recognize your progress. This is where record keeping comes in. On page 18, you will find a Progress Chart. Copy it, put it in a prominent place, and fill it out every week. The information you record on the Progress Chart will come from your Daily Stress Record.

Here is what to do at the end of each week:

- Calculate your average stress level for the week. You can do this by adding up the "average stress" numbers for each day, then dividing by seven. (If you missed a day in keeping your Daily Stress Record, divide by six—but try not to miss a day!)
- Calculate your average highest stress level. Do this the same way, by adding up the numbers from the "highest stress" column on each Daily Stress Record, then dividing by seven.
- Record these two averages on the chart. The numbers in the vertical column from 0 to 8 represent the stress scale. The numbers in the horizontal row from 1 to 15 represent weeks.

After the first week, you will have two results to record on the chart above the number 1. Work out your own system for doing this. For example, you might use a circle to represent your average stress level and an "x" for your highest stress level. Whatever symbols you choose, place them in the appropriate place on the scale. A sample Progress Chart is shown here.

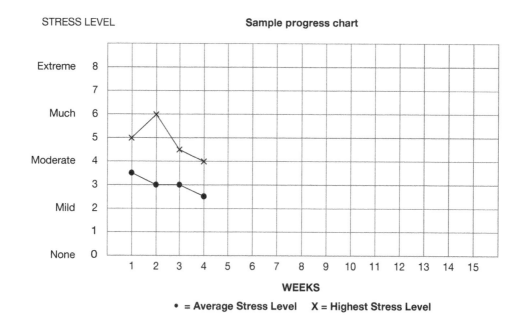

STRESS LEVEL   **Sample progress chart**

• = Average Stress Level   X = Highest Stress Level

TASKS FOR STEP 1

✓ Read this chapter a few times and commit to memory the essential information.

✓ Complete your Daily Stress Record at the end of your day, every day, for two weeks before beginning Lesson 3. (You can move on to Step 2 next week but keep recording.)

✓ Complete your Stressful Events Record during your day, every day, and record each event for two weeks before beginning Step 3.

✓ Complete your Progress Chart at a convenient time at the end of the week for the next two weeks before beginning Step 3.

The Daily Stress Record and the Progress Chart will continue to be a part of your exercises every week throughout the program, so you may want to make multiple copies of them.

Summary

In this lesson we reviewed the role of stress in our everyday lives.

- Stress is a natural, protective response to threats and challenges.
- Different environments can be more or less stress producing.
- Individuals react and respond differently to similar situations.
- These differences may be explained by genetics, and environmental and learned responses.
- The ultimate level of stress you experience will depend on a combination of the event that is producing the stress and your characteristic way of coping with that event.
- We have three basic stress response systems that interact with each other:
  - The physical system
  - The mental system
  - The behavioral system
- We also introduced you to three key records, which will help you understand your own stress:
  - The Daily Stress Record
  - The Stressful Events Record
  - The Progress Chart

Daily Stress Record

$$0 \longrightarrow 1 \longrightarrow 2 \longrightarrow 3 \longrightarrow 4 \longrightarrow 5 \longrightarrow 6 \longrightarrow 7 \longrightarrow 8$$

NONE   MILD   MODERATE   MUCH   EXTREME

Date	Average Stress (0-8)	Highest Stress (0-8)	Stressful Events

Stressful Events Record

0 → 1 → 2 → 3 → 4 → 5 → 6 → 7 → 8
NONE   MILD   MODERATE   MUCH   EXTREME

Date	Starting Time	Ending Time	Highest Stress (0–8)	Triggers	Symptoms	Thoughts

Progress Chart

0 ⟶ 1 ⟶ 2 ⟶ 3 ⟶ 4 ⟶ 5 ⟶ 6 ⟶ 7 ⟶ 8
NONE   MILD   MODERATE   MUCH   EXTREME

STRESS LEVEL

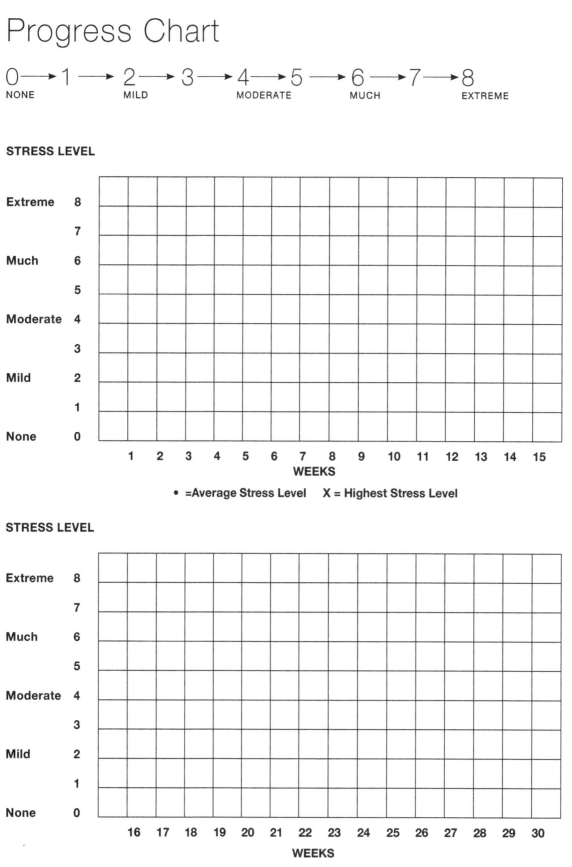

• =Average Stress Level   X = Highest Stress Level

STRESS LEVEL

• =Average Stress Level   X = Highest Stress Level

Relax Your Body

Anyone who has experienced stress (and that's everyone) knows that it can take a physical toll. When you are highly stressed, you spend much of your day feeling and acting tense. Eventually this "hyped-up" state becomes so familiar that you do not realize when you start tensing up. Instead, you feel only the end products of that tension: tiredness, headaches, or possibly back pain. Managing your stress means breaking this cycle of tension. To do this, our first mission is to help you identify the areas of tension in your body and then provide you with techniques to help you reduce that tension.

IDENTIFICATION

Tension, like stress, can be desirable at low levels. For example, you would not be able to write if you could not tense the hand that holds the pen. However, you do not need to tense your whole body, your neck, or your back just to write; your hand is enough. People who have a high level of general stress often tense their entire bodies when they need to tense only one or two muscles. For this reason, it is important to learn to isolate the various muscle groups in your body, so that you will know how each one feels when it is tense.

REDUCTION

Once you have learned how your various muscles feel when they are tense, you will be able to tell when they are tensing up needlessly. This is when you will want to reduce the unnecessary tension. Reducing unwanted tension (relaxation) is a skill that requires a great deal of practice. It is not some sort of "psychological Valium" or a handy crutch you can pull out when you are feeling uptight and then hide away until you need it again. Instead, relaxation must be practiced often—at least once a day at first, for 20 minutes each time. The results will be worth it.

You have probably heard of various relaxation techniques, all with catchy names designed to snare the consumer. Most of them work in much the same way. In fact, you may have already tried some of them. Research has not shown that any particular technique is best for any particular type of person or problem. The deep muscle relaxation technique we recommend here has been studied, researched, and clinically tested and has worked well for many people. Give it a chance to work for you. Remember that this is helping you build a valuable new skill. However, if you have a favorite relaxation technique that works for you, it is quite okay to stick with that. The key is not the particular technique itself—rather it is the regular, consistent practice that is important, together with incorporating relaxation into your life.

The rest of this lesson will show you how to practice deep muscle relaxation. Although no technique is a magic cure for all your troubles, relaxation is an important part of your stress management program.

GETTING READY TO PRACTICE

Think of a sport you enjoy—let's use tennis as our example. Remember how clumsy you felt the first time you tried to hit that ball over the net? If you had quit then, as you might have wanted to, just think of all the pleasure you would have missed. It's much the same with relaxation. You may not "get it" at first; you may feel as awkward trying to relax as you did trying to keep a tennis ball in play. But gradually, if you keep practicing, you will master the skill and become proficient in its use. Before you begin, there are some preparations you can make to create the right environment.

First, choose a time and a place to practice relaxation. If you use a calendar or planner, write it down. Remember to be specific. It is not advisable for you to try and sneak it into spare moments when you are likely to be interrupted. Instead, choose a time when no one else is around or when you can ask others not to bother you for about 20 minutes. Now select a place. Eventually you will be able to do your relaxation anywhere and at any time. But when you are just starting out, make it easy on yourself. Find a quiet room, pull the shades down, turn down the lights, and sit in a comfortable chair. A bed is okay as long as you don't fall asleep. It is difficult to learn when you are sleeping! We recommend you practice the relaxation skill either before your day begins or toward the end of your day. You may need to get up a little earlier or go to bed a little later, but the few minutes of lost sleep will be well worth the effort.

DEEP MUSCLE RELAXATION

Deep muscle relaxation is a process of tensing, then relaxing, individual muscle groups. In this way, you will learn how each group of muscles feels when it is tense and when it is relaxed. You will then learn how to reduce unwanted tension in each one. We will begin with a large number of muscle groups and then, over the weeks, reduce the number, making your relaxation technique shorter and more portable. The chart below lists some of the major muscle groups and suggests ways of tensing them.

12 Muscle Groups: Suggestions for Tensing Muscles
Lower arm: Make fist, palm down, and bend at wrist toward upper arm.
Upper arm: Tense biceps, with arms by side, pull upper arm toward side. (Try not to tense the lower arm; let the lower arm hang loosely.)
Lower leg and foot: Point toes upward to knees.
Thighs: Push feet hard against floor.
Abdomen: Pull in stomach toward back.
Chest and breathing: Take a deep breath and hold it about 10 seconds, then release.
Shoulders and lower neck: Shrug shoulders and then bring them up toward ears.
Back of neck: Press head back against back of chair.
Lips: Press lips together but don't clench teeth or jaw.
Eyes: Close eyes tightly but don't close too hard (be careful if you have contacts).
Lower forehead: Pull eyebrows down (try to get them to meet).
Upper forehead: Raise eyebrows and wrinkle your forehead.

Do you have a quiet room and a comfortable chair? Okay, now you are ready to begin. First, spend a minute or two just settling deeper and deeper into the chair. Breathe slowly and evenly, in and out. Each time you breathe out, picture some of the tension leaving your body, like a bird gliding away. Close your eyes and keep breathing, slowly and smoothly. If closing your eyes makes you uncomfortable, you can start by keeping them open, focusing on one spot on the floor or wall.

When you feel calm and can concentrate, you are ready to start working with your muscles. Keep breathing evenly as you tense and relax each muscle group. Do not hold your breath!

Tense

Begin with your hands and lower arms. As you breathe in, make fists and tense your hands and lower arms. Tense them to about three-quarters of their maximum tension—enough so that the muscles feel tight, but not so much that they are painful.

Isolate

It is important to try to isolate the tension to the one area as much as possible. Therefore, when you tense, make a quick mental check of the rest of your body to make sure that other muscles are not tensing too. For example, when you tense your hands and lower arms, the tension should be restricted simply to these areas. At first, it is likely that you will also tense other parts of your body—your shoulders, stomach, legs—even your breathing may stop. If you notice this happening, try to intentionally relax all parts of your body except for the one or two muscles that you are trying to tighten, and keep your breathing smooth and even.

Concentrate

Keep breathing smoothly and normally. As you breathe, concentrate on the feeling in your hands and arms. Hold the tension for 10 to 15 seconds, about 2 or 3 breaths.

Flop

The next time you exhale, let the tension go. Relax the muscles quickly. You might want to think of your muscles as flopping, the way a rubber band does when you release it. Concentrate on the relaxed feeling. Notice how different relaxed muscles feel from tense muscles? Keep breathing normally. After three breaths or so, your muscles should be completely relaxed. You are now ready to start the process again, with the same muscles.

Break

After you have practiced tensing and relaxing your hands and lower arms two times, take a break for a minute or so. During this time, keep breathing slowly and evenly. Each time you breathe in, count to yourself (1, 2, and so on). Each time you breathe out, say the word "relax" to yourself. Try to picture the numbers and words in your mind as you say them to yourself. If your mind wanders away from the word, let your thoughts go and gently turn it back.

Continue

After a minute or so (around 10 to 12 breaths if you are relaxed), move on to another muscle group. For each group listed in the 12 Muscle Groups chart, repeat the process you used with your hands and lower arms: tensing the muscles for 10 or 15 seconds, then relaxing them for 30 seconds. Keep breathing evenly. Try to tense the muscles as you breathe in, and release them a few breaths later as you exhale. Tense and release each muscle group twice. Each time, focus on isolating the tension, concentrating on the feeling, and letting the muscles flop when you let go. It is important that you take a break after each muscle group, and relax for at least a minute before you start on the next one. These "between muscle" segments are really important and help you to build your concentration and focus away from your worries—a type of meditation. This will help you with a later exercise we will teach you—"staying present".

Your entire practice session should take 20 to 25 minutes. When you finish the last muscle group, give yourself some time to slowly reconnect with the world. Relax all your muscles, then gently open your eyes. See how long you can keep the relaxed feeling as you go about the day's activities.

PROBLEMS WITH PRACTICE

Everyone knows the saying, "Practice makes perfect." When you are first getting started, "perfect" may not describe your practice sessions. Here we will discuss five common difficulties our clients have faced as they began to practice relaxation and suggest ways of dealing with each of them.

Concentrating

Spending 20 quiet minutes alone is a luxury for most people. They have trouble keeping their minds on the task at hand—namely, learning to relax. If you find your mind wandering, do not despair. You are in good company; this is probably the most common problem people encounter and is a particular problem for people who are stressed. It is important to overcome it, however, so that when you are truly stressed, you will be able to clear your mind, concentrate, and relax.

Think of your attention as a muscle. Like any muscle in your body, it becomes weak when it is not used much, and it strengthens gradually as you exercise it. When you start relaxing, you will probably find that you don't get very far in counting your breaths before you start to think of other things—your chores, the kids, what you are doing on the weekend, or your worries. When your attention wanders like this during practice sessions, try not to get angry with yourself. Simply let the extra thoughts that crossed your mind go—release them. You can think about them later; right now, you have more important things to do.

Deliberately turn your attention, as you would turn a car, back to the road of relaxation. Don't worry about what number you were up to—just go back to the number "1" and start counting your breathing all over. The more you do this, the stronger your attention "muscle" will become. Once you start enjoying relaxation and as you become better at concentrating, your attention will wander less often. This exercise will help you get the most out of "staying present," a technique we will introduce you to later.

Isolating Muscles

Some people find it difficult to tense one muscle group while keeping the rest of the body relaxed. The only solution to this problem is the obvious one: Keep trying! Like all skills, this one improves with practice. Try not to be too hard on yourself. You cannot perfectly isolate each muscle group because the muscles in your body are connected. If you have difficulty, lower your standards. If most of the muscles in your body are more relaxed than they usually are, and the muscle group you are working on is more tense than usual, that is fine. But if you find that when you tense your legs, for example, your arms, stomach, face, and breathing all tense up, then you need lots more practice.

Worrying about Time

Some people also find relaxation difficult because the whole time they are trying to relax, they are thinking about all the other things they should be doing. If you have a problem like this, then relaxation is exactly what you need! You purposely need to force yourself to spend time relaxing and, in this way, prove to yourself that the world does not end if you "drop out" for 20 minutes. The work will still be there when you finish, but you need to learn to take time for yourself. The more you do relax, the easier it will be to take time for yourself—worry free.

If you are having trouble stopping your worries or your mind wanders while you are trying to relax, remember to gently turn your thoughts back to your counting and the word "relax" or to concentrating on your muscles. With practice, you will get better at concentrating. If you are worried about spending too much time on your relaxation, you can set an alarm (quietly) for a particular time (say 20 minutes) and then can be assured you won't go over. Eventually, you will find that you are even better at doing your other work when you feel relaxed.

Feeling Frightened

It sounds like a paradox. Some people feel even more stressed when they try to relax. If this is happening to you, it may be because the sensations you feel as your body starts to relax are unfamiliar. You may feel as though you are losing control, and—feeling uncomfortable—you stop. This is perfectly understandable. But it is important to realize that relaxing is not dangerous; in fact, it is healthy. Fear of losing control is one of the main reasons you may be having trouble with stress, so overcoming the fear is important. You may want to try experiencing the feelings of relaxation in gradual steps. For example, start trying to relax with your eyes open, or while a "safe" person is with you.

Consider the example of our case study, Joe. Joe found his work very stressful and spent much of his day in a tensed state. As a result, he often experienced backaches, shoulder pains, and headaches. Obviously, deep muscle relaxation would be a big help to him. But five minutes into his first relaxation session, Joe suddenly jumped up and started pacing. He told us he had felt as if he were falling, and his heart was thumping in a scary way. He didn't like the feeling, so he ran away from it.

We worked out a plan with Joe. He began practicing relaxation by sitting straight up in a chair and keeping his eyes open, staring at a spot on the floor. Gradually he learned to relax this way. He then tried closing his eyes for 30 seconds or so, until he became accustomed to the feeling of relaxing with his eyes closed. Then, gradually, over the weeks, he settled deeper into his chair and closed his eyes for longer periods of time. Eventually he could do an entire 20-minute practice with his eyes closed.

Falling Asleep

Some people have the opposite experience from Joe. They are so relaxed that they fall asleep. If this happens to you, consider it a sign that you may be overtired. Try to get more sleep at night, and try to practice your relaxation at times when you are not as tired, such as the morning. You can also try practicing in a slightly less comfortable setting, sitting in a harder chair or on the floor. Sleep is important, but you are not going to learn much about relaxation if you sleep through your practice sessions.

Trouble Sleeping?

If you have trouble falling asleep at night, you may find that a part of your relaxation exercise can help. Simply use the "counting" part of the deep muscle relaxation. Breathe in and out evenly. Each time you breathe in, let a number (1, 2, and so on) form in your mind. Really concentrate on the number. Each time you breathe out, form the word "relax" in your mind and concentrate on the image of that word. Picture yourself sinking deeper and deeper into the mattress with each out breath. You may have to do this over and over for some time—but try to persist. Worrying about not sleeping is the worst thing you can do. We will help you deal with worrying later. But for now, remember, if worries intrude on your mind, don't get annoyed—just let them go and gently direct your mind back to the counting and the word "relax."

HOW TO PRACTICE

We recommend that you practice your relaxation exercises at least twice a day for the full 20 minutes each time. It is a good idea to keep a record of your practice sessions so that you do not forget or procrastinate and so that you can chart your progress. Try using the **Relaxation Practice Record** on page 28. On this form you can record the date and time of your practice sessions and rate how tense you feel before and after you practice. Using the 0–8 scale, which should be familiar by now, rate the tension and how well you are able to concentrate during practice. Here we have provided Joe's Relaxation Practice Record.

Joe's Relaxation Practice Record

Date	Time	Tension Before (0–8)	Tension After (0–8)	Concentration (0–8)	Comments
9/1	7:30 a.m.	5	6	2	Hard to concentrate—not sure if I'm doing it right.
9/2	1 p.m.	6	4	4	Felt better this time.
9/3	1 p.m.	7	6	3	Too stressed to concentrate.
9/4	8 p.m.	6	3	5	Able to focus more. Lots of tension in shoulders.
9/5	8:30 p.m.	5	3	5	Easier to do it when the kids are in bed.

Gradually, your tension level should drop and your concentration level should rise. If you encounter any problems during a session, or discover any techniques that work especially well, write them down on the chart so you will remember them next time.

In addition to your main practice each day, try to do some "mini practices." When you have a few spare minutes—for example, on your lunch break, in the bathroom, at a traffic light, or during the commercials on television—try tensing and relaxing one or two muscle groups. In particular, work on the muscles that have been giving you the most trouble. Also, as you go through your day, pay attention to which muscles are tensing up, and try to relax them. Sometimes, just doing the meditation part of the exercise (breathing and counting) for 30 seconds or a minute can really help restore a feeling of calm.

TASKS FOR STEP 2

✓ Practice the relaxation technique at least once a day, every day, for at least 3 weeks.

✓ Always fill in your Relaxation Practice Record.

✓ For the first three or four relaxation sessions, reread this chapter before you commence.

✓ Don't forget to use mini relaxations between formal practices.

✓ You may stop filling in your Stressful Events Record, but continue filling in your Daily Stress Record and Progress Chart.

→ Continue on to Step 3 in about a week, but keep practicing deep muscle relaxation.

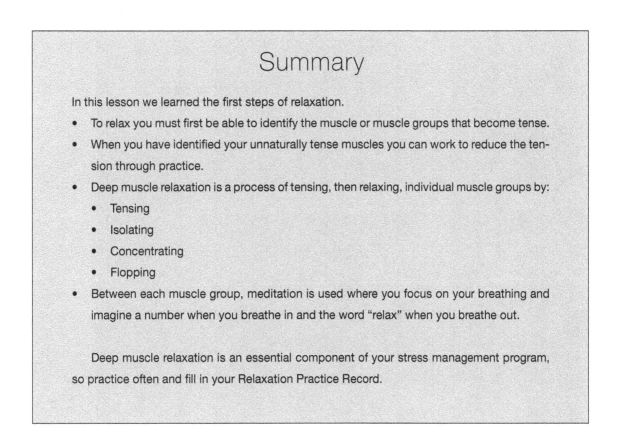

Summary

In this lesson we learned the first steps of relaxation.

- To relax you must first be able to identify the muscle or muscle groups that become tense.
- When you have identified your unnaturally tense muscles you can work to reduce the tension through practice.
- Deep muscle relaxation is a process of tensing, then relaxing, individual muscle groups by:
  - Tensing
  - Isolating
  - Concentrating
  - Flopping
- Between each muscle group, meditation is used where you focus on your breathing and imagine a number when you breathe in and the word "relax" when you breathe out.

Deep muscle relaxation is an essential component of your stress management program, so practice often and fill in your Relaxation Practice Record.

RELAXATION PRACTICE RECORD

0 → 1 → 2 → 3 → 4 → 5 → 6 → 7 → 8
NONE ___ MILD ___ MODERATE ___ MUCH ___ EXTREME

Date	Time	Tension Before (0–8)	Tension After (0–8)	Concentration (0–8)	Comments

Think Realistically

You probably think an event itself determines the way you react to it. That is not true. Actually, your beliefs and thoughts determine how you react. This is why two people can react so differently to the same event. Understanding the relationship between thoughts and reactions is critical to learning to control stress. To illustrate, let's look at an example.

Imagine yourself standing outside a movie theater where a friend has agreed to meet you for the 6 o'clock show. You arrive on time at 5:45, and you stand outside the theater. Try to picture the scene—traffic going by, people walking past laughing and talking, the temperature of the air, and the sounds and smells around you. Imagine yourself pacing slowly up and down, looking at the advertisements, watching other people go in. It's now 5:50, then 5:55, and still there is no sign of your friend. Finally, the clock strikes 6. The last people have gone in, the movie has probably already started, and still your friend is not there. Stop and ask yourself how you would *feel*. What would your actual emotion be, and how strong would it be on the 0–8 scale? Most people report that they would be either worried or angry (maybe around a 6 on the scale).

Now imagine that your friend comes running around the corner and, before you can say anything, says, "I'm so sorry I'm late, but there was an accident right in front of me and I had to help the people while they were waiting for the police and ambulance and my phone has died." Now how would you feel? At this point, most people report that their anger or worry disappears.

If we asked you what *caused* your emotions as you stood outside the theater, you would most likely answer that you were worried or angry *because* your friend was late. But let's look at what happened. Obviously, your friend was late before she showed up. But she was still late even after she arrived. In other words, the event did not change; your friend was late in both cases. However, your emotion changed dramatically. So it could not have been the event that directly caused your emotion. What changed was your interpretation of the event—your beliefs about it. These beliefs are what caused your emotion.

Before your friend showed up, you might have been thinking such thoughts as, "She's always late" or "She's so irresponsible." Those thoughts would have made you feel angry. If you were thinking, "I hope she's okay" or "Maybe she had an accident," or perhaps "Did I come at the wrong time?" you probably would have felt anxious. After your friend arrived and you realized that she was neither hurt nor irresponsible, your thoughts immediately changed. In other words, it was your beliefs about your friend's lateness—not the lateness itself—that caused you to feel worried or angry. If you could have changed your beliefs while you were waiting, you could have saved yourself a lot of unnecessary stress. That is exactly what you will be learning to do in this lesson and the next.

CHANGING YOUR BELIEFS

In order to think realistically, you should understand these five points:

- Your emotional reactions are the direct result of your thoughts and beliefs about an event, not the results of the event itself. Two people react differently to the same event because they think differently about it. Let's say that two men go up in a plane for a skydiving lesson. One man happily jumps out of the plane because he thinks he will experience a great feeling of freedom. The other decides to stay inside the plane because he thinks he might get killed. The relationship between events and reactions is shown below:

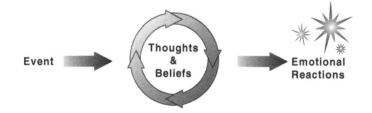

- Extreme emotions are caused by extreme beliefs. By changing your extreme beliefs, you can learn to control your emotional reactions.
- Many of your thoughts and beliefs are automatic, which means that they come very fast and you may not be consciously aware of them. So, it may seem that you just react, without any thought. But the thoughts are really there. It just takes time and practice to identify them.
- Although it is not easy, it is possible to learn to control your thoughts and thus control your emotional reactions. Most people who are troubled by stress believe they have no control over their reactions. But, as we have stated, this simply is not true. Your

thoughts and beliefs are not easy to change; you have spent many years developing them, and they have become a part of you. But you can change them. Once again, the key is practice.

- Realistic thinking is not the same as positive thinking. Positive thinking asks you to look through rose-colored glasses and see the world as a wonderful place. But we all know the world is not always wonderful; this is why positive thinking never lasts long—we tend not to believe it. Realistic thinking, in contrast, asks you to look at situations rationally and objectively. This means that sometimes it is reasonable to feel anxious, angry, or sad. Other times you will notice that your emotions are linked to unrealistic thoughts. When this is the case, the key to changing your emotions is to believe your new thoughts.

OVERESTIMATING PROBABILITY

People who are highly stressed tend to make two types of errors in thinking. First, they overestimate how likely it is that an unpleasant event will happen (overestimating the probability). Second, they overestimate how bad the consequences will be if that event does happen (overestimating consequences). In this chapter we will examine the first of these errors: overestimating probabilities. We will discuss the second in the next chapter.

No doubt you can think of times in your own life when you have overestimated the probability of something bad happening. For example, if your boss says he wants to talk with you, you may immediately think, "He's going to yell at me." If someone cuts in front of you in traffic, you may think, "She did that intentionally." Or if you are asked to take on a new responsibility, you may think, "I won't be able to do it."

In each of these examples, you are assuming a 100 percent probability. By thinking that your boss is definitely (100 percent) going to yell at you, you are thinking that there is no other reason your boss might want to talk with you. Realistically though, there are many reasons your boss may want to talk with you, only one of which involves anger. So you are overestimating.

You may be overestimating even if you don't assume that an unpleasant event is definitely going to happen (100 percent probability). For example, you may not think that you definitely can't do the job, but you may still think that it is very probable that you can't, say 70 percent. But if you have been asked to take on a new responsibility, then at least someone thinks that you can do it.

Overestimating probability does not apply only to worrying. It can also apply to other negative emotions such as depression or anger. If your neighbor is playing his stereo loudly, you may think, "He's just doing this to annoy me." Actually, however, the realistic probability that annoying you is your neighbor's motive is much less than 100 percent and is probably quite unlikely. Imagine if instead of that belief, you thought to yourself, "He may be doing it on purpose (say 5%), but it's more likely he doesn't realize it's bothering me." Think about how much less angry you would be. If you can learn to estimate and think about probabilities more realistically, you can reduce your stress.

CHANGING YOUR ESTIMATES

Identifying Your Thoughts

To change the way you think, you must first learn to identify your thoughts. You can do this by asking yourself questions. Each time you notice your stress level increasing, ask yourself, "What's making me feel this way?" or "What is the bad thing I'm expecting here?" Let's say a business meeting has just been scheduled for this afternoon, and you are worried about it. Immediately ask yourself, "Why am I worried?" If you answer, "Because there is a meeting," remind yourself that events do not cause feelings. Ask a more specific question: "What is it about this meeting that is making me worried—what bad thing am I expecting?" You may answer something like, "I might have to present a report." Now you have managed to identify a belief or, put another way, a negative expectation.

It is important that you be totally honest when you are trying to identify your thoughts and beliefs. Sometimes when you ask yourself a question, the answer may seem so silly that you will not want to admit that you actually had such a thought. But much of our stress is caused by silly beliefs—and they stay with us precisely because we never spell them out and realize how silly they are. So having ridiculous thoughts does not mean that you are crazy. Denying that you have them can hurt more than acknowledging them.

Of course, not all your thoughts will be easy to identify. If you feel an emotion and cannot determine what is behind it, try to guess a few likely thoughts. The simple process of considering and rejecting these possibilities may lessen your stress, or may lead you to the thought that is really causing your emotion.

For example, let's imagine that you came out of a shop to find that someone has double-parked beside you and you cannot move your car. You feel an immediate rush of intense anger. To do realistic thinking means that the first step would be to ask yourself, "Why am I feeling angry?" If you cannot come up with an answer, try and make up a few possibilities: "This person is deliberately trying to make me late," "I am extremely inconvenienced," "This person is trying to take advantage of me in some way." By brainstorming in this way, you might find that one of these thoughts rings a bell and is the main underlying belief that you have in the situation. Even if none of the thoughts rings true, questioning the reality of each one (see below—Looking at Evidence) should help to reduce your anger.

There are two other rules to remember when identifying your beliefs. First, you should try and phrase your belief in the form of a statement. Statements of supposed "fact" are usually responsible for negative feelings, but we often don't realize this. For example, if your house was broken into and you thought to yourself, "I wonder if I've lost a lot?" (a question), you would probably not be too depressed—instead you might be concerned, inquisitive, or curious. These are not emotions that are too stressful. However, if you were to think, "I've lost everything," then you would probably be feeling very depressed or panicky. In other words, extreme, negative feelings generally follow statements of negative events. If you find yourself identifying a curious question as your thought or belief, then you have probably not identified the real thought—in other words, the negative expectation.

Second, for this exercise, you should also try not to let feelings or voluntary actions be the subject of your thoughts. For example, you might ask yourself the question, "Why am I feeling nervous about this meeting?" and might then identify the thought, "Because I will be embarrassed." But remember, embarrassment is not a necessary outcome to the meeting. It will depend on how well you can do your realistic thinking. So looking at how realistic this belief might be is not possible because it will depend on you. Instead, you should ask yourself, "What is it about the meeting that might make me feel embarrassed?" If you then come up with a statement such as, "I haven't prepared my work properly," then this is a clear statement and belief that you can check in terms of how realistic it is. Similarly, if you come up with a thought regarding why you are feeling anxious about the meeting along the lines of, "Because I'm sure I'm not going to say anything," then again this cannot be tested because it is up to you whether you say anything or not. A thought such as "I know I'll say something stupid," on the other hand, can be checked for reality.

Identifying Probabilities

Once you have identified your initial thought, the next step is to ask yourself, "How likely do I really think it is that this will happen?" Usually, the lower the realistic probability, the less intense your emotion will be. For example, if your partner is late and your initial thought is that he or she has had an accident, you will be far more worried if you think there is a 50 percent chance of an accident than if you think there is only a 5 percent chance.

The goal is to convince yourself that the probability of a negative outcome is as low as possible. But you must *really believe* it. If you tell yourself that there is no chance your partner has had an accident, even though you believe deep down that there is a good chance, you will not reduce your level of stress. The key is to change your actual beliefs, not simply to change what you say to yourself. To help to really convince you that you are overestimating, you need to learn to look at realistic evidence for your beliefs. By learning to always check your thoughts against the evidence, you can start to think much more realistically. There are four types of evidence that will help you.

General Knowledge

The first way for you to identify real evidence about a belief is to consider all of the facts, figures, and general rules about a situation. For example, what have other people told you about this situation, what have you read, or what have you heard through the media? One warning—everyone thinks they know the difference between real evidence and wild imaginings. But people who are highly stressed tend to ignore the positive evidence and focus only on the negative. You need to look out for this tendency in yourself. Try consciously to focus on *all* of the evidence, not only on the negative.

Say your partner is late and you are trying to determine the realistic probability that he or she has been involved in an accident. You may ask yourself, "How many cars are on the road in the city tonight?" Perhaps you estimate 10,000 cars. Then, based on your rough knowledge of accident rates, you may ask yourself, "How many of those cars are likely to have an accident tonight?" Perhaps two. That means there is a 2 in 10,000 chance that your partner will have an accident—no doubt much lower than you originally thought.

You might have a tendency to say, "Yes, but I always think that my partner will be one of the two." This is precisely what we mean when we say that your thinking needs to stop being based on "gut feeling" and to begin to be based on realistic evidence. You need to look at all of the evidence and realize that your partner has about the same chance of being in a car accident at any given time as you have of winning the lottery!

Previous Experience

Another good way for you to challenge your estimates is to try and look at previous experiences you have had in that situation. For example, with your partner who is late getting home, you might ask yourself, "How many times in the past has my partner been home late?" "How many of those times were because of an accident?" "Is my partner generally a good driver?" "Would I have heard by now if he or she had been in an accident?" Your answers to these questions will probably help you to further reduce your estimate of how likely it is that your partner has been in an accident.

Remember again not to focus on the negative. Maybe your partner did have an accident once and came home late. But what about the 50 times he or she has been late for other reasons? If you focus on the one time and ignore the 50, you are not thinking realistically. Chances are, once you have examined *all* the evidence, your initial thought will not seem nearly as likely as it did at first.

Alternative Explanations

Another way to learn to think more realistically is to think of all the possibilities, not just the one that initially worries you. For example, why, apart from an accident, might your partner be late? List the possibilities: he or she got caught in traffic, had a flat tire, met some friends, or maybe had to finish a project at work. You know your partner's habits. Does he or she often lose track of time? Does he or she like to work late because the office is quiet after others go home? Clearly, an accident is only one of a large number of possible reasons for your partner's lateness. There is little use in focusing on one negative possibility if so many other events are equally possible.

By examining the realistic evidence and listing all the possibilities, you should be able to convince yourself that, while your partner may have had an accident, the probability is actually very, very low. If you really come to believe this (by convincing yourself with evidence), your stress will decrease.

Changing Perspectives

Finally, a good way of looking at realistic probabilities is to try and see the situation from a different perspective—usually, someone else's. For example, if the situation were reversed and you were the one who was late coming home, would you expect your partner to be stressed? Why not? The answer to this question will often help you to see how unrealistic you are being and will help to change your view of the situation.

Changing perspectives in this way is a good strategy for finding evidence relating to social situations. These situations are often difficult to examine in other ways. There are usually no statistics or written facts about social situations. For example, imagine that two colleagues are talking loudly outside your office. You may feel angry and identify a thought such as, "They are totally inconsiderate." Now try to change perspectives—imagine that you are one of the people talking in the corridor and one of the colleagues is in his office. Are you talking loudly because you are totally inconsiderate, or could there be something else going on—perhaps you don't realize how loud you are? By putting yourself in the other person's place in this way, you can often reduce your extreme feelings very quickly.

RECORDING YOUR THOUGHTS

No one said it would be easy to change your thoughts. It is not enough to read through this lesson and say, "Okay, I'll think more realistically in the future." Your negative thoughts are deeply ingrained in you; they come automatically before you can stop them. If you want to replace them with realistic thoughts, you will have to make a commitment to regular, formal practice. The way to do this is to write down your thoughts and then challenge each one. To challenge a thought means to look at all of the evidence for it and then decide how realistic it is based on that evidence. Writing out your beliefs may seem tedious at first, but it is the best way to identify and examine them objectively.

The form to use for this step is the **Realistic Thinking Record**, a form for recording your thoughts and your responses to them. This form is a bit trickier than the others you have used, and it is important that you use it correctly. If you read the instructions below carefully and consider the examples and case studies that follow, you will soon be an expert at using the form.

- In the first column, record the event—the thing that triggered your negative feelings. Include only the event, not your feelings about it. For example, in this column you would put "job interview tomorrow," not "doing badly at the job interview."
- Next, record your initial expectation, thought, or belief. Ask yourself, "What is it about this event that bothers me?" This then is the belief that is directly leading to your negative feeling. Remember to be totally honest about identifying this belief, even if it sounds silly. Remember, also, to phrase this belief in the form of a statement and to try not to include feelings or actions that are up to you.

- The most important column is the evidence. Here you need to list all of the evidence you can think of that supports or does not support your belief. Because this is realistic thinking (and not positive thinking), you do need to record even evidence that supports your belief. Hopefully, if you are being honest and are thinking hard, you will find more evidence against your belief than for it. However, when you do this exercise, you might occasionally find that your beliefs are realistic. In this case, the exercise might be telling you that it is quite understandable to feel stressed about this situation and perhaps you need to deal with it in a different way, such as trying to change the situation.

When you are listing the evidence, try to think of each of the four types of evidence we discussed—general knowledge, past experience, alternative explanations, and changing perspectives. Not all types of evidence will fit for all situations, and you may need to be clever and think up other types for some situations. Remember to watch out for biases in your thinking. Make sure you look at all of the evidence, not just the negative.

- Once you have carefully evaluated all of the evidence for your belief, you should record the realistic probability that the outcome you are thinking about will occur. Take what you have written in the second column and ask, "Realistically, how likely is it that it will happen?" We hope that if you take into account all of the evidence, this probability will not be as high as it was when you began the exercise.
- Now that you have determined the realistic probability, how intense is your emotion about the event? Record that number in the last column using the 0–8 scale that you should now be familiar with. Ideally, having determined the realistic probability should make the intensity lower than it was when you began the exercise. But, remember, your emotion will only change if you believe your new probability. If you are simply saying a low probability to yourself, but believe deep down a higher probability, your emotion will stay high.

WHEN TO DO THE EXERCISE

If you do not find your emotion changing, don't despair. This is not an easy technique, and it will take lots of practice. It will not start to work overnight. We will also learn lessons in later weeks that will help the realistic thinking to work, and we will also continue on to the second part of realistic thinking in the next lesson. So, at this stage, your aim should be to practice the realistic thinking technique, not necessarily expect it to work completely. We hope you will start to see some effects from it, but there will be later additions that will help.

The Realistic Thinking Record is designed to be filled out each time you notice yourself reacting emotionally to an event. Make lots of copies of the record and carry it with you. When you feel your stress rising, fill out the form immediately if you can. If you can't, do it as soon as possible—no later than the end of the day. Write down your thoughts and examine the evidence for each one.

You should not wait for major stresses to use the technique. Remember, at this stage your main aim is to practice. Therefore, you should grab the opportunity to use the form whenever you notice any degree of stress, no matter how small.

Your ultimate goal is to reach a stage where you automatically interpret events realistically, rather than automatically seeing them in a negative way. In other words, you will eventually be able to do your realistic thinking while the event is happening. At first, however, most people stumble through a stressful event any way they can, then sit down later to try to think more realistically about it. This will not reduce your stress during the day, but it does give you practice. Next time, you will be able to start your realistic thinking a little sooner.

If, like most of us, you have some continuing worries or aggravations—money, your children's health, job pressures, an annoying work colleague—practice realistic thinking on those as well. Long-term stresses provide a good chance to try to change your thinking during the event—in other words, while you are stressed, instead of later.

ANNE

Anne wanted her daughter Ellie to start preparing some of the evening meals. But when she thought about approaching Ellie with this request, she felt very anxious (6 on the 0–8 scale). The first step was to try to identify her negative expectation. To do this she asked herself, "What is it about asking Ellie that worries me?" Her answer (her initial expectation) was that Ellie would get angry. Anne realized that she was assuming there was a strong chance that Ellie would get angry, and as soon as she recognized that thought she knew she was overestimating.

Anne then considered the evidence for her initial expectation. She considered her previous experiences and recalled a time when she'd asked Ellie to clean the bathroom. Ellie didn't look exactly overjoyed, but she wasn't angry. Anne told herself, "It's a reasonable request that she help out," and "Most adults who live in the same house share the chores." Next, she looked at alternatives, at how Ellie might respond. "Maybe she'll be happy to help," thought Anne. "Or maybe she won't be happy but still agree that it's a fair request." Finally, Anne tried to reverse positions and imagine what she would say if she were the one being asked to help out more at home. Anne knew straightaway that she would see what a fair request it was, and try her best to fulfill it.

Anne realized that her estimated probability of Ellie being angry (80 percent) was much too high. She decided that the realistic probability was more likely 20 percent. This new way of looking at the situation helped her stress level decrease, from a 6 to a 3. You can see that Anne was being realistic: she still thought there was a reasonable chance that Ellie would get angry, and so she still felt a little nervous. But she managed to reduce her estimate from 80 percent to 20 percent, and this helped her to go from feeling really scared to a little nervous. Below is Anne's Realistic Thinking Record for her work situation as well as other examples from her week.

Anne's Realistic Thinking Record

Event	Expectation (Initial Prediction)	Evidence (How Do I Know?)	Probability (Realistic)	Emotion (0–8 Scale)
Want to ask Ellie to prepare dinner sometimes.	She will get angry.	She doesn't like cooking much. She has agreed to do housework before without being angry. It's a fair request. Most adults share housework. She might be happy to help.	20%	3
Electricity bill due Monday.	We can't afford it. It will be cut off.	We do have less money than we used to. We don't spend as much as we used to. We still have some money in the bank. I can phone the company and ask for a payment plan if I need to.	10%	2
Steve seemed distant at work.	He thinks my report wasn't good enough.	He often seems distant—that is the way he is. He might have a lot of other things on his mind. He didn't say anything about my report. The report seemed OK to me.	10%	2

JOE

Joe had been with his wife in a restaurant where the waitress had forgotten their order and kept them waiting for 30 minutes before Joe finally asked what was happening. Joe had blown up at the time and had then spent the rest of the evening in a bad mood. Although he did not do his realistic thinking at the time, Joe's wife encouraged him to do it that night, as a practice. When Joe asked himself what it was about his order being forgotten that triggered his anger, he identified his main initial belief as, "The waitress is incompetent." Joe then tried to examine the evidence that the waitress was incompetent just because she forgot the order. His main evidence was found when he looked at alternative explanations for the order being forgotten. Joe realized that maybe the waitress had been extremely busy, maybe some major event had happened to distract her, or maybe some major issues in her life had made her particularly distracted tonight. He also changed

Joe's Realistic Thinking Record

Event	Expectation (Initial Prediction)	Evidence (How Do I Know?)	Probability (Realistic)	Emotion (0–8 Scale)
Waitress forgot order.	She's incompetent.	She forgot the order. The restaurant was very crowded—she was probably really busy. She might have been stressed by something else. She apologized. She brought the bill immediately when we asked for it.	40%	4
Heavy traffic on way to work.	I'll be late.	The traffic is heavy at least twice a week. I have been (slightly) late for work a total of three times in the past year. I leave plenty of time to get to work, even with heavy traffic.	10%	3
Argument with Mel.	She is totally unreasonable.	She was upset. She is usually a reasonable person. She finds it hard to talk about some things calmly. I lose my temper too sometimes.	15%	4

positions with the waitress mentally and realized that, if it had happened the other way around, he would expect a customer to accept a single mistake and that one mistake does not mean a person is generally incompetent. Weighing up this evidence, Joe realized that there was a slight to moderate chance that the waitress was incompetent, but it was not 100 percent as he had originally felt. Below is Joe's Realistic Thinking Record.

TASKS FOR STEP 4

✓ Practice recording your thoughts and estimating realistic probabilities for at least one week on the Realistic Thinking Record.

✓ Record your thoughts and probabilities as soon as you notice your stress level increasing.

✓ At the end of the day, think of any instances in which you overreacted to an event but did not have a chance to record it. Record your thoughts and challenge them as if they were happening right now.

✓ Continue to fill in your
  ✓ Relaxation Practice Record
  ✓ Daily Stress Record
  ✓ Progress Chart

➔ You can move on to Step 4 in about a week if you feel that you are getting the hang of realistic thinking. If you feel unsure in any way, reread this chapter and keep practicing for a little longer.

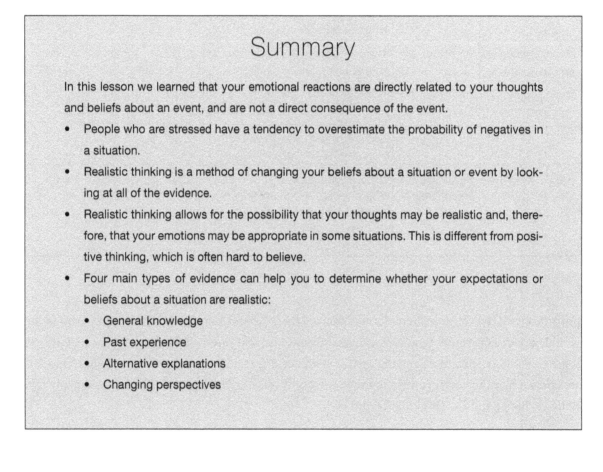

Summary

In this lesson we learned that your emotional reactions are directly related to your thoughts and beliefs about an event, and are not a direct consequence of the event.

- People who are stressed have a tendency to overestimate the probability of negatives in a situation.

- Realistic thinking is a method of changing your beliefs about a situation or event by looking at all of the evidence.

- Realistic thinking allows for the possibility that your thoughts may be realistic and, therefore, that your emotions may be appropriate in some situations. This is different from positive thinking, which is often hard to believe.

- Four main types of evidence can help you to determine whether your expectations or beliefs about a situation are realistic:
  - General knowledge
  - Past experience
  - Alternative explanations
  - Changing perspectives

Realistic Thinking Record

0 —→ 1 —→ 2 —→ 3 —→ 4 —→ 5 —→ 6 —→ 7 —→ 8
NONE   MILD   MODERATE   MUCH   EXTREME

Event	Expectation (Initial Prediction)	Evidence (How Do I Know?)	Probability (Realistic)	Emotion (0–8 Scale)

Evaluate Consequences

Welcome back. After a week or more of practicing realistic thinking, you should feel yourself making progress. You may still overestimate the probability that bad things will happen, but chances are that your estimates are becoming more realistic every day. While you keep working on that skill, it's time to tackle the other misunderstanding in thinking that is common to people under stress: overestimating the consequences of a negative event. You might think of it as making mountains out of molehills.

To highly stressed people, life seems to pack a double whammy. They believe that unpleasant events are likely to happen, and they believe that if those events happen, the consequences will be absolutely horrible. People who "catastrophize" automatically expect the worst possible outcome. For example, if these individuals are awakened by a noise in their house at night, they may immediately assume that it is a burglar who is going to harm or kill them. If they are called into the boss's office, they immediately think they are going to be fired.

Most people who assume the worst are unaware they are doing it. Since they have never stopped to identify the consequences they are imagining, the consequences stay at a subconscious level, where they cannot be disproved. In other words, the unrealistic consequences are like the unrealistic probabilities we discussed in Step 3. They lurk in the darkness of your mind, ready to do harm, until you bring them out and see them for what they are.

WHAT WOULD HAPPEN IF...

You can identify the consequences you assume by asking yourself a simple question: "What would happen if the thing I am worried about really took place?" As we said before, realistic thinking is not purely positive thinking. We have to admit the possibility that negative things can happen. The last lesson showed you that the chance of these negative things happening is often far less than you might have thought, but still there is a chance. So the next step is to accept that chance and then ask yourself: "If the negative thing I expect did occur, what would really happen?" The answer to this question will produce the expected consequence of your first belief. As you will see, this expected consequence will simply be another negative expectation. Therefore, you are now in a position to examine the realistic evidence for this second belief. In most cases, you will find that the consequences would not be nearly as bad as you first assumed. The same rules apply to the consequence as to the initial expectation—try to phrase it as a statement and try to stay away from feelings or voluntary actions.

Let's return to the example in which your partner is late getting home and your first thought is that he or she has had an accident. When you think realistically, you may realize that the chance of this is very small—less than 1 percent. But that's still a chance. So, your next step is to ask yourself, "What would really happen if my partner did have an accident?"

At this point you will be doing something that may or may not come naturally, talking to yourself. You do not have to do it aloud—although there is nothing wrong with that if it makes you feel more comfortable. All you have to do is ask yourself questions and then answer them. Although talking to oneself has a bad reputation, it is actually very useful. You should get into the habit of mentally asking and answering questions as you practice realistic thinking.

When you ask yourself what would really happen if your partner had an accident, you might immediately answer, "He or she would be killed." What does this answer remind you of? Right—it is an overestimation of probability, and you know what to do with those! It is obvious that most accidents are not serious enough that they kill or maim people. It should now be obvious that overestimations of consequences are simply overestimations of probability that lie below your original thoughts—sort of like the layers of an onion.

Asking yourself, "What would really happen if…?" or "So what if…?" is just another way of identifying your next thought. Many people find that asking these questions opens a sort of Pandora's box, with one thought leading to another and another. It is important to keep going and identify all your thoughts, no matter how frightening or silly they seem, until you reach the bottom of the box.

If you think realistically, you would eventually learn to cope even if your partner were hurt or killed in an accident. This may sound callous, but it is a realistic fact. Humans can cope with an amazing amount of difficulty. When you reach the answer that is at the bottom of all the questions you are asking yourself, you will usually find that it is not the end of the world, as you feared.

The following examples show the kind of questioning we have been discussing. Our first case, about Rhani, is a good illustration of how one question can lead to another and another until the bottom line is reached. In these examples, the questions are asked by experts, but you can do the same kind of questioning yourself.

RHANI

Rhani had a customer who seemed unhappy with the beauty treatment that Rhani provided.

RHANI: I'm worried that she will call or write to my boss to complain.

PROFESSIONAL: How likely is it that she will do that?

RHANI: I know it's not very likely. If she was going to complain, she probably would have done it at the time of the treatment. If she wasn't happy she'll probably just take her business elsewhere. The likelihood of her bothering to call or write is probably only 5 percent.

Note: Rhani has been doing Step 3 for a week or two and is clearly able to look at evidence for her initial belief quite quickly.

PROFESSIONAL: Let's assume she does call to complain. What would happen?

RHANI: My boss would fire me.

PROFESSIONAL: It sounds like you are assuming there's a 100 percent probability that your boss would fire you. How likely do think that really is? Try and look at some evidence.

RHANI: Hmmm. . . . I'm generally a good beautician. I know of other customers who have complained and the people who did their treatments didn't get fired. It wasn't as though I did anything wrong—I think the customer just had unrealistic expectations about the results of the treatment. I can explain that to my boss . . . if she'll listen. So, when I look at all the evidence, I guess it's not that likely that I would get fired—maybe 10 percent.

Note: See how the professional treated Rhani's first consequence to her initial thought as simply another overestimation of probability and asked Rhani to examine the evidence for it, which Rhani is now very good at doing.

PROFESSIONAL: Okay. But let's not stop there. What would happen if you did get fired?

RHANI: That would be awful.

PROFESSIONAL: Why? What would really happen?

RHANI: Well, I'd be out of work. Who knows if I'll ever find another job.

PROFESSIONAL: I've noticed that you just made a prediction there. You essentially said, "I'll never find another job." Could you take some time to think through the evidence for that?

RHANI: Well, I'm not sure. It didn't take me too long to find this job, I suppose. So it might not take that long to find another one. But the job market is not as good as it used to be. That said, I do have a couple of friends from beauty college who found work recently. So, I don't really know the probability of not finding another job, but it's definitely not 100 percent like I first thought.

PROFESSIONAL: And what would happen if you didn't find another job?

RHANI: I guess I'd have to move back in with my parents until I found something. I wouldn't like that, but I guess it wouldn't be the end of the world. I could use the opportunity to do some extra study so I could get a better job next time.

PROFESSIONAL: So, in other words, putting all that together, there seems to be only a small chance that the customer will complain to your boss. And even if they do, there's only a small chance that you would get fired. And even if you did, you may well find another job quickly, and even if you didn't, you would survive. So it doesn't sound as bad as it first seemed. How much stress do you feel now?

RHANI: Not much at all. When you put it that way, it isn't nearly so stressful.

ERIK

Erik had an assignment due the next day and was worried that he would not get it done on time.

ERIK: I'm so disappointed in myself. I really wanted to get everything in on time this semester, but I can't get this done by tomorrow.

PROFESSIONAL: How much have you done?

ERIK: I have done lots of research and have written a draft. But it needs to be completely rewritten.

PROFESSIONAL: What would happen if you handed it in as it is?

ERIK: I'd get a bad mark.

PROFESSIONAL: Have you ever gotten a bad mark before?

ERIK: Well, I've failed a few times, but that's only been when I haven't handed the assignment in at all. Whenever I have actually managed to submit the assignment, I have gotten a really good mark.

PROFESSIONAL: Have you ever submitted an assignment you didn't feel happy with?

ERIK: Lots of times. I'm basically never happy with what I submit. I always think it could be better.

PROFESSIONAL: What feedback have you had from your teachers about your work?

ERIK: They say it's excellent. But they also say I need to be more consistent with handing things in on time.

Note: Here the professional has been asking Erik to look at different types of evidence—particularly, his past experience and the general knowledge he has about his marks.

PROFESSIONAL: So then, looking at all the evidence, how likely do you think it is that you would get a really bad mark, like a fail mark, if you were to hand in the assignment tomorrow?

ERIK: Oh, I guess about 10 percent. But I'd feel terrible. I hate knowing that I could have done better.

PROFESSIONAL: Okay. Now let's assume that you do feel terrible after handing it in. What would happen?

ERIK: What do you mean? I'd feel terrible—that's bad enough!

PROFESSIONAL: You mentioned earlier that you are usually unhappy with work you submit because you think it could be better. In your experience, how long does that terrible feeling last?

ERIK: Well, actually, it is usually only really terrible for a few minutes. Then I get distracted by the next thing I need to do and I forget about it until I get the assignment back.

PROFESSIONAL: And how do you feel when you don't hand something in on time?

ERIK: I feel really guilty and disappointed in myself. And that feeling actually drags on for a lot longer.

PROFESSIONAL: So again, how bad would it be if you felt terrible after handing something in?

ERIK: It wouldn't be so bad—I know the feeling only lasts a few minutes, and it is a lot better than if I don't hand anything in at all. Plus, I'd be a step closer to finishing my degree.

JOE

Joe's mother calls him frequently, often interrupting him while he is busy with work or other tasks.

JOE: My mother is always calling just when I'm in the middle of doing something important, and it makes me so angry, I find that I get short with her.

PROFESSIONAL: Let's try and look at what you just said in a more realistic way. When you say that she always calls in the middle of something, it implies 100 percent of the time. Is that true? How likely is it really that she will call when you are doing something important?

JOE: Well, I suppose that when I think back over the last 10 times she's called, most of the times I was just watching TV or reading. There was once when I was making dinner and it burned because she interrupted me. Another time, I was busy with some work I had brought home from the office and she called. I guess that makes it 20 percent of the time.

PROFESSIONAL: OK, great. That's the first part. Now let's go a bit further. Ask yourself, "So what if she calls at an inconvenient time?"

JOE: Well, I know that one of my first thoughts is that she doesn't think anything I do is important. But, before you say anything, I know that is a major overestimation since she obviously doesn't know what I'm doing when she calls. However, I suppose I also think that it's a major interruption and inconvenience to have to stop at that point.

PROFESSIONAL: A major inconvenience sounds pretty extreme. What is the evidence that it is so major?

JOE: When I was doing my work, I forgot what I was up to and it took me 10 minutes to work it out again. I guess that's not so bad—it's only 10 minutes. And when the dinner burned, it was really not too bad, just a little burned. Part of that was my fault anyway, because I could have turned the stove down before I went to the phone.

PROFESSIONAL: So, it sounds like, even when she does interrupt, it is an inconvenience, but maybe not such a major one.

JOE: True. And I know what you are going to say next. Even if it is a major inconvenience, it's not the end of the world. I have handled plenty of bigger problems than this at work.

In questioning Erik, Rhani, and Joe, the professional was challenging them—challenging the probability that negative events would happen and challenging the likelihood of the dire consequences they imagined. Below are some additional tips for thinking realistically, so that you can learn to challenge your own thinking, just as a professional might.

CHANGING PERSPECTIVES

Learning to think realistically means learning to see things objectively. One way to move toward this goal is to try looking at your situation from someone else's point of view. We have already discussed this technique as one way of gathering evidence to determine realistic probabilities. But the technique can be used in a broader way, and it is so useful that it is worth describing in more detail.

Think about the people you know. Is there a person whose calm, logical manner you have always admired? Someone who never seems to lose his or her cool, no matter what happens? You have a choice. You can let people like that drive you crazy or you can get pointers from them. Choose the calmest person you know and try to find out how his or her mind works. Because everyone likes compliments, you may want to start by saying something like, "You know, I've always admired the way you stay calm in upsetting situations. How do you do it?" Chances are, the person will be glad to talk. Or perhaps you already know the person well enough to know the attitudes that keep him or her on an even keel.

Let's say that the calmest person you know is Lee. After you have talked to Lee, experiment with seeing the world from Lee's perspective. The next time a stressful event happens, ask yourself, "What would Lee think about this?" Or try imagining that the event has happened to Lee instead of you. What would you think about that event if you knew that it had happened to Lee? If Lee came to you asking for advice, what would you say? It's possible that you would give very good, useful advice to other people but have trouble knowing what to do when you are in a similar situation yourself. Putting yourself in someone else's shoes works especially well in three areas that worry people under stress: social concerns, perfectionism, and anger.

Social Concerns

Social concerns is a name for something that everyone does: worry about what other people think of you. For some people, this kind of worry can become so intense that they become afraid to do anything. If you tend to worry too much about other people's opinions of you, try pretending to be those other people. Let's say, for example, that you bump into a coworker in the supermarket and introduce your spouse—but you call your coworker by the wrong name. Immediately, you feel embarrassed. Because you have practiced realistic thinking, you know that your embarrassment comes from a thought, probably something like, "That person must think I'm totally stupid." Now turn the situation around and imagine that your coworker had introduced you by the wrong name. Would you have thought he or she was completely stupid? Probably not. And even if you did feel bad about it for a minute, you probably would have laughed about it the next time you saw your coworker, right? So by reversing positions, you have come up with easy evidence to help lower the probability of the statement, "That person must think I'm stupid."

Perfectionism

The desire to do things perfectly causes as much stress in many people as worrying about what others think. Logically, we all know that no one is perfect. Unconsciously though, we often believe that we should be. Again, putting yourself in someone else's shoes is a good way to gather evidence against such thoughts.

For example, if your boss asks you to do a special project, you may immediately begin to worry that your performance will not be good enough. The worry probably results from an unconscious thought such as, "It will be a disaster if I make even one mistake." But what if one of your colleagues at work did the same project and made a few small errors? Would that really be terrible? Would you think that your colleague was a hopeless case and should be fired? Of course not. You would probably think, "It's too bad about those mistakes, but everyone makes them, and overall that person did a good job." Once again, reversing positions has shown you that the probability of your original thought—that any mistake would be disastrous—was really very low.

Anger

Many people under stress have a tendency to become angry and irritable for often totally irrational reasons. In many cases, they may hold unconscious beliefs that others are stupid or nasty, and that they themselves are battling everyone else's incompetence. In such cases, putting yourself in another person's position is a good way of gaining perspective and being able to understand and forgive minor mistakes in others. For example, let's assume you are driving to a meeting and you are a little late. Suddenly, in front of you, a car changes lanes and then proceeds to drive quite slowly. Your immediate response may be to get angry and to start sounding your horn. These responses are probably being produced by thoughts along the lines of: "That jerk!"; "He's totally inconsiderate!"; "He's purposefully trying to make me late!"; and so on. Now try to put yourself in the front car's position. Have you ever driven anywhere slowly, perhaps because you were looking for something or your mind was preoccupied? Do you always carefully watch all of the other cars when you are in a hurry? By gaining this perspective, you may then be in a better position to do your other realistic thinking and realize that by driving behind this car you are only going to arrive at your meeting a few seconds later than you would have anyway.

EVALUATING CONSEQUENCES

You have already been challenging your probability estimates, using the Realistic Thinking Record. We now want to introduce you to a new Realistic Thinking Record, shown on page 00.

Rhani's Realistic Thinking Record

Event	Expectation (Initial Prediction)	Evidence (How Do I know?)	Probability (Realistic)	Emotion (0–8 Scale)	Consequence
Unhappy customer.	She'll complain to my boss.	If she were going to, she would have done it on the day. She probably won't bother and just go somewhere else next time.	5%	4	I'll be fired.
	I'll be fired.	I'm a good beautician. Other customers have complained, and no one got fired. The customer had unrealistic expectations.	10%	3	I won't find another job.
	I won't find another job.	Found this job easily. Job market not as good now, but I do know others who've found work. Could live with parents till I get something.	2%	1	I could survive.

The first five columns of this new form are just like the old one. You will record the objective event, your initial expectation about it, the realistic evidence for your expectation, the realistic probability that what you expect will actually occur, and your emotional intensity. Then, to complete the final column, ask yourself, "What would happen if the negative thing I expected actually did occur?" or "So what if my initial belief is true?" As we discussed earlier, this will help to identify your expected consequence. Write that consequence in the last column. But wait! You're not done yet!

Below the place where you wrote your initial thought, write the consequence again. This is important because you now need to look at the evidence for your expected consequence. Now start the whole process over as if that were your initial thought. In other words, challenge this consequence just the way you challenged your initial thought. After you have looked at all of the evidence and come up with a realistic probability for this second level, ask yourself, "What would happen if this new possibility (my previous consequence) really occurred?" In answer to this, you might come up with another consequence. Record it in the consequence column (below the first), then start a separate line and again write that consequence back in the initial expectation column (now your third expectation). You then need to challenge that consequence as an initial thought—that is, look at evidence and so on. Keep on going until you can't go any further. This usually happens when you can't think of any other consequences, or you reach zero emotion. At the end, you should read back over the whole exercise and realize just how unlikely it is that anything really bad will happen. Remember that the likelihood of each consequence depends on the likelihood of the belief before it. For example, if you decide there is a 1 percent chance that you will lose your job after making a mistake and then decide that if you lose your job, there is a 10 percent chance that you will not get another one, the overall chance that you will be out of work is 0.1 percent—that is, 10 percent of 1 percent—or, almost none!

The process will become clearer if you study the sample below that reflects Rhani's case discussed earlier in the lesson. As you can see, a single event has the potential to produce a page or more of thoughts. Make several copies of the Realistic Thinking Record, and do not be afraid to use as many as you need. Eventually you will not need the sheets at all; you will be able to do all of your challenging in your head. But as with all the other skills you are learning, this one takes practice.

TASKS FOR STEP 4

✓ Use the new Realistic Thinking Record on page 52 for at least the next three weeks to practice challenging your probabilities and your consequences.
✓ Remember:
  ✓ Follow your chain of thoughts as far as you can, no matter how silly some of your thoughts seem.
  ✓ Fill out the sheet during or as close to the stressful event as possible.
  ✓ Carry a few sheets with you, and get into the habit of turning to them. Soon it will become second nature.
✓ Continue to fill in your
  ✓ Relaxation Practice Record
  ✓ Daily Stress Record
  ✓ Progress Chart

Summary

In this lesson we continued our exploration of realistic thinking.

- We emphasized the importance of continuing your thought process beyond your "initial expectation" and looking at your expected consequence.
- This expected consequence can then be seen as a new belief that can also be challenged by looking at all of the evidence.
- Some events or situations will result in many layers of beliefs.
- We presented case examples to illustrate how this process takes place.

Realistic Thinking Record II

0 →1 →2 →3 →4 →5 →6 →7 →8
NONE   MILD   MODERATE   MUCH   EXTREME

Event	Expectation (Initial Prediction)	Evidence (How Do I Know?)	Probability (Realistic)	Emotion (0–8 Scale)	Consequence

Test Predictions

Pause for a moment and think about what you have been doing the last few weeks. Can you see the progress you have made in challenging your unrealistic thoughts? Do you feel as if you have taken at least a small step toward controlling your emotions? Progress in mastering stress is more subtle than progress in other areas of self-improvement, such as losing weight. If you have lost weight, friends are likely to stop you on the street and exclaim, "Oh, you look so much thinner!" They are far less likely to stop and say, "Oh, you seem so much calmer!" Eventually the change will be obvious to those closest to you.

For now, though, you should be careful to give yourself credit. Take time out now and then to read over your recording forms, think about recent events, and pat yourself on the back for your progress. If you feel you are progressing too slowly, you may be expecting too much. Even so, it is a good idea to go back to basics by rereading Chapters 3 and 4, and practicing. This is good advice even if you seem to be going great guns. It may help to brush up on the details. Once you have mastered the basics of realistic thinking, you are ready to start testing predictions.

PREDICTION TESTING

By now it should be almost second nature for you to ask yourself, "How likely is it?" when you notice a stressful thought. To come up with a realistic probability, you need to take into account as much realistic evidence as possible. But people who are stressed often have trouble assessing evidence; they focus on the negative and ignore the positive. Take our case example, Rhani.

Rhani wanted to attend a friend's birthday party at which she knew only a couple of people. She was anxious about attending because she thought that she would have no one to talk to and appear out of place. Rhani had trouble finding evidence to challenge this thought. When she got to the party she did end up talking to a range of people, but she was so focused on her anxiety, and the times when she felt awkward, that she came away from the party convinced that her negative thoughts were true.

You can see that Rhani's tendency to focus on the negative prevented her from looking objectively at what had actually occurred when she went to the party. To help her look at the evidence more realistically, we suggested that Rhani try a technique called prediction testing for her next social event. In prediction testing, you predict what you think will happen in a certain situation. You ask yourself beforehand: What evidence will I need to look for to see if these predictions come true? Then, when it's over, you compare your predictions to the evidence you collected. Doing this over and over will give you an accurate perception of reality, based on real evidence.

The next time Rhani attended a party, she made similar predictions. She predicted, "I will have no one to talk to," and "People will think I don't belong." We asked her to consider how she would know if her predictions came true. That is, what evidence would she need to look for? Rhani found this a challenging question. Normally, she just focused on her own feelings and used these as evidence—if she felt awkward, she assumed she looked awkward. But we didn't accept this and encouraged her to consider the facts. How would she really know if her predictions came true?

The first prediction was easy enough to test. She would count the number of people she talked to. If the number turned out to be zero, she would know her prediction was correct. The second prediction was more difficult. How would she know what other people were thinking? Like the rest of us, Rhani could not read minds—although she often tried to! We encouraged her to look only at the most reliable evidence. Did anyone say she looked out of place? Did anyone ask her what on earth she was doing there? Rhani agreed to take note of these facts, and competed the first three columns of her **Prediction Testing Record**:

Event	Predictions—What Do I Expect to Happen?	Evidence to Look For— How Will I Know If My Predictions Come True?	Outcome—Did My Predictions Come True?
Janet's party.	I will have no one to talk to. People will think I don't belong.	Count—how many people do I talk to? Observe—does anyone say I look out of place or that I don't belong?	

Rhani then went to the party and looked for the evidence she needed. When she got home, she recorded the outcome in the final column of her Prediction Testing Record:

Event	Predictions—What Do I Expect to Happen?	Evidence to Look for—How Will I Know If My Predictions Come True?	Outcome—Did My Predictions Come True?
Janet's party.	I will have no one to talk to. People will think I don't belong.	Count—how many people do I talk to? Observe—does anyone say I look out of place or that I don't belong?	No. I talked to seven different people. No one said I didn't belong, or anything like that.

Prediction testing allowed Rhani to observe what *actually* happened at the party, and evaluate her predictions based on these facts. The next time she went to a party, Rhani was able to recall the experience and use it as evidence as she did her realistic thinking.

Prediction testing is an extremely powerful tool for reducing stress and building confidence over the long term. In order to get the most out of it, complete the following steps, using your Prediction Testing Record. The first three steps need to be completed *before* you enter the stressful situation.

1. Write down the event or situation that you are feeling stressed about.
2. Write down your predictions—what do you expect to happen?
3. Write down the evidence that you will need to look for in order to work out whether your predictions come true. It may be useful to ask yourself, what would convince someone else that your predictions are correct? This step can be the most difficult part of prediction testing, but it is vital. Take time to think it through *before* you enter the stressful situation.
4. Go into the situation and observe all the evidence that you identified in step 3. This will require you to focus on what is actually happening around you, not just your own feelings of stress.
5. Write down the outcome. Using the evidence you collected, were your predictions true or not?

Using this method, you will probably find that most of your stressful predictions do not come true. This will provide you with excellent real-world evidence that you can use in future realistic thinking. Occasionally, however, you may find that your stressful predictions do come true. If this is the case, don't despair—you have discovered useful information. Now that you know that you *were* thinking realistically, you are in a better position to use some of the other strategies in this program, such as Problem Solving, which is outlined in Chapter 10.

For more examples of prediction testing, let's consider the cases of Erik and Anne.

ERIK

Erik was stressed about submitting an assignment because he didn't think it was good enough and was concerned that he would fail. In order to test this prediction he had to wait until he had received his grade. But he didn't stop there. He also asked his teacher directly for feedback about the quality of his assignment. This helped him to get a realistic perspective of what he had done well, and what he could improve next time.

Erik's Prediction Testing Record

Event	Predictions—What Do I Expect to Happen?	Evidence to Look For— How Will I Know If My Predictions Come True?	Outcome—Did My Predictions Come True?
Submitting assignment.	It isn't good enough. I'll fail.	Look at my grade. Ask my teacher for feedback.	No, I passed. My teacher said it was well researched. She said I could improve it by changing the structure.

ANNE

Anne was trying to reduce her stress by having lunch in the park instead of at her desk. However, she found that her stressful thoughts about what would happen if she left her desk, even for just half an hour, kept her in the office. Anne decided to commit to at least one lunch in the park, and test her predictions. You can see her Prediction Testing Record Form below:

Anne's Prediction Testing Record

Event	Predictions—What Do I Expect to Happen?	Evidence to Look For— How Will I Know If My Predictions Come True?	Outcome—Did My Predictions Come True?
Eating my lunch in the park instead of at my desk.	I will fall behind with my work. Others in the office will think I'm lazy.	Are any important tasks left undone at the end of the day? Does anyone in the office say anything about me being lazy or not getting enough done?	No. I still finished what I needed to. No one said anything—I don't even think they noticed.

As you can see, prediction testing allowed Erik and Anne to find out whether their stressful predictions actually come true or not, based on real-world evidence. Approaching situations in this way allows you to evaluate your predictions on the basis of fact as opposed to a "hunch" or a general feeling. One of the difficulties of prediction testing, however, is that people often try to avoid those situations that might give them the best evidence. In Rhani's example, evidence could be gained by going to the party and seeing what happened. But if, as many shy people do, Rhani had avoided the party altogether, it would have been difficult for her to collect the evidence she needed.

WHY IS AVOIDANCE A PROBLEM?

Everyone knows that the best way to learn something is to experience it firsthand. How many parents complain that their children have to learn from their own mistakes? Yet most of us tend to avoid the types of situations that have caused us stress in the past, and we therefore never learn to deal with them. Additionally, if we avoid, we never get the opportunity to test our predictions. Avoidance stops us from finding out that perhaps things aren't as bad as we expected.

Of course, it is natural and normal to wish to avoid something that causes you stress. But it is important to recognize that such avoidance makes your stress much worse in the long term. You may be able to see this by thinking back to a situation that you felt stressed about in the past. Perhaps you started a new job, or went on a plane for the first time. It is natural that that situation would have caused at least a little stress. But what happened to that stress as you went back to that job week after week, or continued to fly on planes? Most likely your stress levels dropped. You discovered that it was OK, that you could cope, and you got used to the situation.

Now imagine that you hadn't returned to that job after the first day, or that you had refused to get on the plane. What would have happened to your stress? In the short term, it probably would have improved—there would have been the instant relief of not having to face the situation. But over the long term, it would have gotten much worse. You would still be stuck with the belief that the job was too hard, or that the plane would crash. The next time you tried to start a new job or board a plane, your stress levels would be even higher than before.

What Do You Avoid Because of Your Stress?

There are many situations that people avoid due to their anticipation of stress. We have listed some of the common ones below, but we would need a whole other book to cover them all. The best way to identify what you avoid is to observe your own behavior. Asking a trusted friend or relative for their ideas might also help.

Commonly avoided situations (place a check next to those you avoid):

☐ Medical appointments
☐ Speeches

- ☐ Presentations
- ☐ Job interviews
- ☐ Participating in meetings
- ☐ Parties or social events
- ☐ Getting injections
- ☐ Saying no
- ☐ Delegating tasks
- ☐ Taking time for yourself
- ☐ Asking for help
- ☐ Plane travel
- ☐ Driving
- ☐ Elevators
- ☐ Catching trains or buses
- ☐ Staying overnight away from home
- ☐ New places

Another kind of avoidance that commonly occurs is when a person does a behavior too much to try to avoid stress. For example, our case study Erik would check his e-mails several times before sending them because he was so worried about making a mistake. This checking was unnecessary and wasted a lot of time. Because Erik always checked his e-mails so many times, he never learned that the chances of his making a mistake were actually small and that, even if he did make a mistake, it was probably not the end of the world. When Erik stopped checking his e-mails over and over, he quickly realized that he almost never made mistakes, and, even when he did, he was not yelled at and did not lose his job. In this way, Erik learned not to worry as much about making sure his work was absolutely perfect and also became more efficient at doing his work. This reduced a huge part of his daily stress.

Another example of an excessive behavior can be seen in our case study Joe. Joe was so concerned about being late that he always left far too much time to get to appointments. This meant that he was usually very early and would waste time waiting for the person he was meeting (who was sometimes a little late). This made him irritable and even more stressed. We suggested that Joe stop leaving so much time to get to appointments, and even try being deliberately late. Although this was initially stressful for Joe, he was able to find out that when he allowed less time he was still rarely late. Finally, he discovered that even if he was late, it wasn't the end of the world—others understood because they were sometimes late too.

Are there any behaviors you do excessively because of your stress? We have listed some common ones below. Place a check next to those that apply to you:

- ☐ Check work too much
- ☐ Ask others for a lot of reassurance that what you're doing is okay
- ☐ Spend too much time on tasks, trying to do it "perfectly"

☐ Stick to routines that are too rigid or inflexible
☐ Leave too much time to get to places, due to worry about being late
☐ Spend too much time making sure things are neat or clean
☐ Be excessively careful with money

Take note that all these behaviors can contribute to stress when they are *excessive*. Of course there is nothing wrong with generally trying to be on time, keeping things clean, or sticking to a budget. The problem occurs when you do this behavior excessively, and feel stressed when something prevents you from doing it. Remember in Steps 3 and 4, when we suggested the technique of Changing Perspectives to help you with your realistic thinking? This technique involves choosing a calm and rational person in your life, and asking yourself how he or she would think if he or she were in your situation. Changing Perspectives can also be useful in identifying your own excessive behaviors. If the calm, rational person you know is called Lee, ask yourself, "Would Lee check his e-mails five times before sending?" or "Would Lee spend 45 minutes making sure his hair is perfect every morning?" If you don't know, ask him! The answer to this question will help you to determine if your behavior is justified or excessive.

GETTING STARTED

Once you have identified some situations that you avoid, or some behaviors that you do excessively, it is time to start prediction testing. Do the opposite of what you would normally do. If you would normally avoid going to the party, go to the party and start a conversation with someone. If you would normally rush around making the house look perfect before friends come over, leave it looking messy. And then, test your predictions. Use your Prediction Testing Record Form and observe the evidence—what really happens?

If It Seems Too Difficult

As we have already discussed, prediction testing is stressful. You may well say, "I'm reading this book to reduce my stress, not increase it!" And, of course, you are right. The catch is that prediction testing is an extremely powerful tool for reducing stress *in the long term*. It is only in the short term that your stress will be increased.

If doing the opposite of what you would normally do seems too stressful to bear, we suggest making change slowly and gradually. If it seems too stressful to go to a big party, you could try going to some smaller social gatherings first. If spending only 5 minutes on your hair in the morning seems impossible, then first try spending only 10 minutes. The important thing is that you make some change, and use your Prediction Testing Record Form! As you collect more and more evidence about what really happens, you will feel more comfortable about making bigger changes.

To conclude, we will illustrate this principle of slow and gradual change with our case study, Rhani.

RHANI

Rhani had been feeling unhappy at work for a long time. She had tried to change her own reactions to her boss's frequent criticisms, and although this helped a bit, Rhani longed to work for someone more friendly and supportive. Friends and family often urged Rhani to look for another job, but Rhani felt highly anxious about the prospect of a job interview. Whenever she thought about interviewing for a job a range of negative predictions came to mind, such as "I won't be able to answer the questions," "I'll stammer over my words," and "I won't get the job."

Rhani knew that she should test these predictions out by going to a job interview, but she just felt too anxious to try. So, she decided to test her predictions in a slow and gradual way. First, she did an Internet search for common job interview questions, and then wrote out a list of questions she thought she would be asked. Then she had her sister ask her the questions, just as if she were in a job interview.

Even though this was just a role-play at home, Rhani still found it stressful. But she was able to test her predictions, as you can see from her record below:

Rhani's Prediction Testing Record

Event	Predictions—What Do I Expect to Happen?	Evidence to Look For—How Will I Know If My Predictions Come True?	Outcome—Did My Predictions Come True?
Job interview role-play at home.	I won't be able to answer the questions. I'll stammer over my words.	Count how many questions I can answer. Ask my sister to give me feedback about whether I stammered.	Mostly no. I could answer seven out of the eight questions she asked. She said I stammered a little bit at first but sounded much more confident once I had gotten through the first question.

Rhani used this evidence to help her think realistically about job interviews. Due to her high level of stress, she decided to continue practicing with role-plays at home, working up to practicing in front of her whole family. Each time she used her Prediction Testing Record Form. After several practices, Rhani felt confident enough to attend a real job interview and, after a few interviews, eventually got a new job. Even though it had initially been quite stressful, Rhani was glad that she had pushed herself to test her predictions. By doing so she discovered that she could perform well, get a new job, and take control of her life.

TASKS FOR STEP 5

✓ Your main task for this chapter is to start prediction testing. Make sure you use the Prediction Testing Record. The first three steps need to be completed *before* you enter the stressful situation.

1. Write down the event or situation that you are feeling stressed about.

2. Write down your predictions—what do you expect to happen?

3. Write down the evidence that you will need to look for to determine whether your predictions come true. It may be useful to ask yourself, what would convince someone else that your predictions are correct? This step can be the most difficult part of prediction testing, but it is vital. Take time to think it through *before* you enter the stressful situation.

4. Go into the situation and observe all the evidence that you identified in step 3. This will require you to focus on what is actually happening around you, not just your own feelings of stress.

5. Write down the outcome. Using the evidence you collected, were your predictions confirmed or not?

✓ If you are avoiding situations due to your stress, start facing them and use the Prediction Testing Record to test your predictions.

✓ If you are doing a behavior excessively, start reducing this behavior and use the Prediction Testing Record to test your predictions.

✓ Prediction testing is normally a bit stressful in the short term, but it is very effective in reducing stress over the long term. If it seems too hard, start making changes using small steps, slowly and gradually. Don't forget to use your Prediction Testing Record for every stressful situation you encounter.

✓ If you are finding it difficult to get started with your first step, you may want to reread the introduction to the book, where we talked about motivation.

✓ Keep filling in your
  ✓ Daily Stress Record
  ✓ Progress Chart

✓ You can stop filling in your Realistic Thinking Records at this stage if you don't feel you need them. But you need to make sure that you still carry out realistic thinking in your head. Go back to using the sheets any time you have difficulty.

✓ You can also stop using your Relaxation Practice Records if you wish. However, you should still include regular practice of relaxation, especially mini-relaxations, as an ongoing part of your life.

Summary

In this lesson we introduced the technique of prediction testing to help provide you with even more realistic evidence. In prediction testing, you predict what you think will happen in a certain situation. You ask yourself beforehand—what evidence will I need to look for to see if these predictions come true? Then, when it's over, you compare your predictions to the evidence you collected. By doing this over and over, you get an accurate perception of reality, based on real-world evidence.

Many people avoid situations that they find stressful. This can be a problem because they never get a chance to test their predictions. Avoidance provides short-term relief but increases stress over the long term. Often, a person will do a behavior (such as checking or cleaning) excessively to try to avoid stress. This is a form of avoidance, and also leads to further stress in the long term.

Prediction Testing Record

Event	Predictions—What Do I Expect to Happen?	Evidence to Look For—How Will I Know If My Predictions Come True?	Outcome—Did My Predictions Come True?

Stay Present

One of the key features of stress is that it grabs your attention and focuses it on the source of threat. As discussed in Step 1, this is a helpful process if you are in immediate physical danger. However, if you are not in immediate physical danger, the tendency to focus on perceived threat is not beneficial—it just makes you more stressed. Often, when people are stressed, they are focused on things that *might* happen in the future (for example, not getting work in on time, being late, being disapproved of, or being embarrassed). If you look over your Realistic Thinking Records, you will probably see lots of these future-focused thoughts.

Sometimes stressful thoughts might not be concerned with the future, but rather focused on the past. It may be that you experience significant stress when thinking about events that have already occurred. This may be because you think the event shouldn't have happened, and you blame yourself or someone else. Perhaps you rehash the event over and over in your mind, thinking about how you could have handled it differently. Or it may be that you are worried about the consequences of the event, taking you once again to future-focused thoughts.

Either way, we know that chronically stressed people are often absorbed in either the future or the past. Realistic thinking is a technique to ensure that your thoughts about the future or past are realistic, both in terms of probability and consequences. However, some people also find it useful to simply change the focus of their attention. Rather than focusing on the future or the past, they choose to focus their attention on the present moment, that is, what is actually happening around them right then and there.

You have already had some experience with present-focused attention in two of the earlier steps in this program. The first experience would have been in Step 2, when you learned deep muscle relaxation. Remember, the "break" minute between muscle groups, when you focus on your breathing? This develops your ability to stay focused on the present moment and to let all other thoughts and distractions go. You may find this part of relaxation to be a challenge. If so, don't be concerned—in this step we introduce a technique for making it a little easier.

Your second experience of present-focused attention would have occurred in Step 5—prediction testing. When testing predictions you usually need to focus on what is actually going on around you, in order to gather the evidence you require. So, even though it is different from relaxation, prediction testing also involves present-focused attention. If you are carried away with thoughts about the future or the past, you will not be able to test your predictions accurately.

MINDFULNESS

In this chapter, we build on these earlier experiences of present-focused attention, and introduce a new technique that you can use in almost all stressful situations. You may have heard of the concept of mindfulness. Mindfulness meditation is an awareness practice that derives from Buddhism. One of the defining features of mindfulness meditation is that it involves present-focused attention. Western psychologists have taken the concept of mindfulness and adapted it for treating stress, anxiety, and depression, with good results. Mindfulness meditation has also been found to have significant benefits for people with physical health problems such as chronic pain and coronary heart disease.

Many books have been written on mindfulness meditation, and it is not within the scope of this book to address it in depth. However, we will present some simple tips, taken from mindfulness, to help you stay in the present moment.

Staying Present

1. Start by focusing on your breathing, just like in your relaxation exercise. Breathe slowly and evenly. Notice the rise and fall of your chest and stomach as you inhale and exhale.
2. Now use your five senses. Ask yourself, "What can I see, hear, smell, feel, and taste—right now?" Notice the details. Pretend you are describing it to someone who has never seen, heard, smelled, felt, or tasted it before.
3. Notice when thoughts distract you. These thoughts might be the typical worries you often experience. Or they might be thoughts about the exercise itself, such as "Am I doing this right?" or "This is silly."
4. Let those thoughts go. Make a decision not to engage with them right now. You can think about them later if they are important.
5. Refocus your attention. Return your attention to your breathing, and then use your five senses again. You may need to refocus many times as your mind wanders—don't be distressed by this. Refocusing once your mind has wandered is a key part of the process.

Two of our case studies, Joe and Anne, found staying present to be a particularly useful skill. The following descriptions show how they put it into practice.

JOE

Joe noticed that he often felt highly stressed on the drive to work. He had completed a Realistic Thinking Record and knew that he spent much of the drive thinking about how bad the traffic was, predicting that he would be late for work, and worrying about all the work he had to get done. Joe knew that many of his predictions were unrealistic and unhelpful. For example, he knew that he was usually not late for work, and that even if he was late it wouldn't matter very much. He also knew that the traffic was outside his control, and that no amount of stress and agitation on his part would make it move any faster.

Despite this realistic thinking, Joe still found the drive to work a stressful experience. He decided to practice staying present during the journey, hoping that this would help. In order to steady himself, Joe began by focusing on his breathing. He took slow and steady breaths, focusing on the rise and fall of his chest as the air flowed in and out. Next, Joe used his five senses to keep him fixed in the present moment. For example, he noticed that the clouds outside were dark gray in the center, with fluffy white edges. He became aware of each vehicle around him and his position on the road. Joe paid attention to music on his stereo and identified the separate sounds of the guitar, drums, and keyboard. He noticed the faint taste of toothpaste in his mouth.

Joe noticed the feel of the steering wheel in his hands and became aware that he was gripping it tightly. He used his relaxation training to let the tension go, and noticed the impact of this on his hands, arms, and shoulders. He became aware of several odors in the car—gasoline, coffee, soap.

As he was practicing being in the present moment, Joe also noticed some of the same old worries creeping back into his mind. At first Joe found these distracting. It was hard not to get carried away with his usual worrying thoughts. It took him some effort to let them go and refocus on the present, which he did by returning his attention to his breath. Once again, Joe used his five senses to anchor him into the present moment. He repeated this process time and time again, returning to his breath every time he noticed a distracting thought.

By the time he arrived at work, Joe felt considerably less stressed than usual. He was also reminded of how much he enjoyed music when he really listened, and resolved to dig out some of his old CDs after work.

ANNE

Anne had taken a useful step toward reducing her stress by committing to a half-hour walk after work most evenings. However, she was disappointed to find that it didn't help as much as she'd hoped. Anne usually walked with a sense of urgency, keen to get the walk over with so she could get on with other things at home. Anne's Realistic Thinking Record revealed frequent thoughts such as "This is a waste of time," "This isn't helping," and "I really should be doing X." Often she felt even more tired and irritable by the time her walk was over.

Rather than giving up, as she was tempted to do, Anne decided to practice staying present during her walks. Instead of judging whether the walk was worthwhile or not, Anne focused her attention on her breathing, and what was actually around her. She really noticed the colors in the sunset, the salty smell of the nearby lake, and the crunch of leaves underfoot. As soon as she became aware of the usual worries about home and work, Anne reminded herself of her wish to stay present, just for this half hour. She then returned her attention to her breath and used her five senses again. Anne focused on what she could see (yellow and orange leaves, the muddy path, her own feet), hear (birdsong, a dog barking, the shouts of a child), feel (a breeze against her cheek, the soft lining of her coat pockets in her hands), smell (a fire burning, salt, her own perfume), and taste (apple). For the first time, Anne actually enjoyed her walk.

PERSISTENCE IS KEY

As you can see, both Joe and Anne used their breath and their five senses to anchor them into the present moment. This didn't mean that their usual worries didn't intrude—of course they did. But Joe and Anne patiently kept returning to their five senses time and time again, resulting in a significant reduction in their stress.

One analogy that can be useful is to think of your mind as a distractible puppy you are taking for a walk. You want the puppy (your mind) to stay on the straight and narrow path of the present moment. The puppy, however, wants to head off in all different directions, sniffing a future tree here and a past bush there. There is no point getting upset with the puppy, as it is just behaving as all puppies do. Instead, it is your job to notice when the puppy is heading off course, and gently tug it back onto the present path. If you remain patient, and keep doing this time and time again, the puppy will soon be spending more time in the place you want it to be.

CONQUERING THE MAGIC OF WORRY

What? There's magic in worry? Not really, but plenty of people seem to think there is. When you worry, all the possible outcomes to a situation swirl around and around in your mind. Often the thoughts keep swirling even when you know there is nothing you can do to change the situation you are worrying about. It's almost as if you believe that worrying will magically change the out-come. That is the so-called magic of worry. In other words, some people almost seem to believe that they must worry over things, just in case there is something that they have missed or forgotten.

This belief probably comes from the human need for control. Most of us have trouble accepting the idea that there are some things in life that we just cannot control. Rather than accepting this reality, we keep worrying, unconsciously hoping that somehow the worry will change things. This belief may not be conscious, but the worry is. Breaking the worry cycle requires you to accept the fact that you cannot control everything. Some events are going to happen whether you want them to or not, whether you worry about them or not. Your worrying will have absolutely no effect on these events. But it does have an effect on you; it can make your life very unpleasant.

Our case study Anne illustrates this principle well. Anne often worried about her daughter when her daughter stayed out late at night. She knew that her daughter was a grown, capable woman and that it was unlikely anything terrible would happen. But she felt that, by worrying about her daughter, she could reduce the chances of a negative event. Anne described a "magical" belief about the power of her own thoughts: "If I worry about it, it won't happen." This belief got in the way of Anne's efforts to stay in the present. On the one hand, she wanted to worry less, but, on the other hand, worry made her feel safe. So naturally it was hard for Anne to let these worries go.

It was only when we questioned this "magical" aspect of worry that Anne was able to recognize how unrealistic, and unhelpful, her beliefs about the worry process were. Logically, she could see that worrying would have no impact whatsoever on the potential events that could befall her daughter. Some people would drive dangerously, whether Anne worried about it or not. Others would commit crimes, regardless of what Anne thought about as she lay in bed at night. It was hard to accept, but Anne had to realize that she could not protect her daughter from all the bad things in the world.

Anne eventually accepted that she did not have control over what happened to her daughter. But she realized that she did have control over her own thoughts, and her own stress. Anne decided to focus on the life that was taking place all around her, not the imaginary life in her mind. Once she made this decision, it was much easier for her to use her breath and five senses to stay in the present moment.

It may sound simplistic just to tell yourself, "Don't worry." But worrying is like any other habit; the first step toward breaking it is becoming more aware of it. When you are aware that you are worrying, you can make a conscious decision to return your attention to the present moment. If you need reinforcement, try putting up signs. For example, you may want to make yourself a large sign that says, "Return to the present!" and tape it to your refrigerator to remind you. Or put a reminder in your phone for times that you know you are most likely to worry.

PRACTICE—ANYTIME, ANYWHERE

Like all the other techniques outlined in this book, staying present is a skill that takes practice. But don't be concerned. Practicing this skill won't take any extra time out of your day! Staying present can be practiced while you are going about your usual business. For example, you could practice staying present while driving to work or taking a walk, as in the case studies above. Or you could practice while doing everyday chores, such as doing the laundry, brushing your teeth, or watering the garden. Use your imagination. There is no end to the activities during which you could practice this skill!

To help you practice, use the **Staying Present Record**. Complete this form after each practice.

In the first two columns, record the date and time you practice. This will allow you to see how regularly you are practicing.

In the next column, record the activity you are doing as you practice.

Next, write down any present-focused observations you made. That is, anything you noticed with your five senses. You probably won't be able to note down every small detail that you noticed, but that's OK. Just note down the ones you easily remember.

Finally, write down any thoughts of the present or past that you noticed while you were practicing. Remember not to worry if you have these thoughts while you are trying to stay present. Just notice them and return your attention to what is around you, using your five senses.

Joe's Staying Present Record

Date	Time	Activity	Present-Focused Observations	Thoughts of Past or Future
9/30	8 a.m.	Driving to work.	Clouds, cars around me, music, feel of the wheel in my hands, coffee, gasoline.	Will the traffic speed up? Meeting later today—will it go well? Wondering how my mother is doing.
10/1	7 p.m.	Watering the garden.	Crickets chirping, soft grass underfoot, cold water, smooth feel of the hose, fading light, pink rose blossoms, dark green leaves, droplets caught in spider's web, smell of meat cooking.	Argument with Mel this morning.... Why is she so sensitive? What time is the game on this weekend?

Anne's Staying Present Record

Date	Time	Activity	Present-Focused Observations	Thoughts of Past or Future
7/17	6 p.m.	Walk.	Leaves, colors, mud, my feet, birdsong, dog, shouts, perfume, salt, soft fabric, apple, fire, sunset	Work, will Ellie be OK? Memories of when we first moved here
7/18	8 p.m.	Washing dishes.	Lemony detergent, foamy bubbles, tinkling sounds as the dishes touch, spiky fork, sound of laughter from next door, clock ticking, my breathing, heat of the water, steam on my glasses.	Why was the car making that sound this morning? What if Jon doesn't find work again?

TASKS FOR STEP 6

Staying Present

✓ The steps for staying present are:

1. Start by focusing on your breathing. Breathe slowly and evenly. Notice the rise and fall of your chest and stomach as you inhale and exhale.

2. Now use your five senses. Ask yourself, "What can I see, hear, smell, feel, and taste—right now?" Notice the details. Pretend you are describing it to someone who has never seen, heard, smelled, felt, or tasted it before.

3. Notice when thoughts distract you. These thoughts might be the typical worries you often experience. Or they might be thoughts about the exercise itself, such as "Am I doing this right?" or "This is silly."

4. Let those thoughts go. Make a decision not to engage with them right now. You can think about them later if they are important.

5. Refocus your attention. Return your attention to your breathing, and then use your five senses again. You may need to refocus many times as your mind wanders—don't be distressed by this. Refocusing once your mind has wandered is a key part of the process.

✓ Remember that staying present takes persistence. It is normal to be distracted by thoughts and worries. The key is to notice when your mind has wandered and use your breath and five senses to return to the present, time and time again.

✓ Keep filling in your
   ✓ Daily Stress Record
   ✓ Progress Chart
   ✓ Prediction Testing Record

Summary

In this lesson we introduced a technique for staying present.

People who are stressed often spend much of their time thinking about possible threats in the future or the past. By focusing on the present moment, that is, what is actually happening around you right now, you can reduce your stress.

Staying Present Record

Date	Time	Activity	Present-Focused Observations	Thoughts of Past or Future

Take Control

Consider the words of the Greek philosopher Epictetus: "Some things are up to us and others are not." This may seem obvious, but it is an important message for everyone trying to reduce stress in their lives. When a person spends all her energy trying to change things that are beyond her control, stress levels rise immensely. Equally, when a person believes there is nothing he can do—that he is entirely a victim of circumstance or other people—this also leads to stress, and great unhappiness. One of the key tricks in managing stress is to figure out what you have control over, and what you don't. When you know this, you can then direct all your efforts toward the things you can control, leading to maximum satisfaction and minimum stress.

This is not a new idea by any means. As mentioned, it was central to the thinking of Epictetus, back in the first century AD. You may also have heard of the Serenity Prayer, often read at Alcoholics Anonymous meetings. Regardless of the religious component, this also captures the same key principle. It says, "Lord, give me the serenity to accept the things I cannot change, courage to change the things I can change, and the wisdom to know the difference."

These ideas are the focus of this chapter.

THINGS YOU CANNOT CHANGE

There are some things that you clearly cannot control, and you probably spend very little time worrying about them. The weather is one example. Most of us probably prefer sunshine to clouds and rain, but accept that this is absolutely beyond our control. When it rains you may feel disappointed, but rather than getting upset about it, you simply focus on what you can control (wearing boots, taking an umbrella) and move on with your day.

Other less obvious aspects of life are also beyond your control. One example, which many people spend a lot of time worrying about, is what other people think. It is natural to desire the acceptance and approval of others, but at the end of the day what others think is up to them, not you. You have some control over your own behavior when interacting with others. You can decide to be friendly or hostile, respectful or disrespectful. But, however you behave, this will not guarantee that others will like you or think well of you. The way other people think is shaped by many factors completely outside your control—their personality, their culture, their upbringing, their beliefs, their current mood. You have little to no influence over these factors. Accepting this fact will lead to far less stress over social and interpersonal concerns.

And, of course, there are a thousand other factors that will affect your life but that you cannot control. This is the simple reality of life. You cannot control the economy; you cannot control the natural environment. The aging of your body, your baby's tendency to wake through the night, the traffic, your neighbor's decision to renovate his house (again)—all these factors are beyond your control. It can be a little scary to think about this reality. In some ways it is easier to pretend that, if we just do everything right, everything will go our way. But most of us know this is not true, and a simple viewing of the evening news will confirm that bad things do happen—even to good people. The old adage, "Life wasn't meant to be easy," captures the notion that all of us will endure hardship at some point in our lives.

So, how do you manage stress when so many things are beyond your control? What if you are in a genuinely stressful situation, facing problems such as poor health, financial hardship, or relationship difficulties? The answer to this question is to focus on the things that you *can* control in your life. Decades of research indicate that when people focus on what they can control, they feel less stressed. Many psychological programs, from those that assist people in coping with traumatic events and chronic pain to those aimed at building resilience in military personnel, make this a cornerstone of their approach. So, when you are feeling stressed, it is important to ask yourself, "What can I control here?" The answer to this question will vary from situation to situation, but a few key areas are a good place to start. These are discussed below.

THINGS YOU CAN CHANGE

Your Thoughts

Epictetus, the Greek philosopher, argued that one thing we all have control over is our own beliefs. This idea is the foundation of cognitive therapy, on which much of this book is based. No matter the situation, it is always worthwhile to identify and reflect on your thoughts by doing the realistic thinking exercises described in Steps 3 and 4. In our treatment clinic, we see many instances when a person makes an objectively difficult situation much worse by thinking about it in an unrealistic and unhelpful way. Try not to fall into this trap. Use your realistic thinking skills to be as rational as you can in even the most challenging situations.

Our case study Rhani illustrates the way this can be done. Several weeks into her therapy with us, Rhani's fiancé suddenly called off their engagement. Rhani was very much in love with him and had no idea that he was unhappy. So, when he suddenly ended their relationship, Rhani was understandably deeply distressed. The loss of a valued relationship can be one of the most painful human experiences, and so naturally it took Rhani some time to grieve and move forward in her life. But, even in this normal adjustment process to a very stressful event, Rhani still benefited from identifying and challenging her thoughts.

Over the months following the breakup, Rhani was able to identify the thoughts that caused her the most distress. These were, in essence, "There must be something wrong with me" and "I'll never find love again." Gradually, both on her own and with her therapist, Rhani examined the evidence for these thoughts and considered alternative points of view. Eventually, Rhani made a list of more realistic thoughts, including, "We both made mistakes in the relationship," "The breakup has been very hard but I have learned a lot," "I am not alone—many people I know have had relationships end," and "It is highly likely that I will fall in love again in the future." This change in perspective made a big difference to the way Rhani felt. She still missed her fiancé, but thinking realistically helped her to cope much better with this difficult time in her life.

Your Attention

Early in this program you learned to strengthen your attention by practicing regular relaxation and meditation, and hopefully you are still practicing, at least from time to time. In the previous step, we also described the technique of staying present. This technique is extremely useful for situations in which you have little control over what is going on around you. You may recall that Joe used it when he was stuck in traffic—a potentially stressful situation that many people find themselves in every day. When you are stuck in traffic you can't do anything to change the traffic itself, but you can choose where you put your attention. You can focus on negative predictions ("I will be late," "My boss will be furious"), or you can accept that there is little you can do and let those negative thoughts go. Choosing to stay present, rather than getting carried away with stressful thoughts about the future, is a simple way of taking control.

Our case study Anne found this to be an invaluable tool when she had to undergo some important medical tests. As she waited for the test results to come back, Anne was consumed by anxious thoughts about the future. What if the tests indicated a serious health problem? How would she, and her family, cope? Anne was understandably stressed because she was facing a potentially serious situation, and she had very little control. She couldn't control when the tests would come back or, more important, what they would say about her health. So Anne decided to exert control over something she could influence—her attention. When she began to have catastrophic thoughts about the future, Anne reminded herself that these thoughts were just ideas about the future, not reality, and that worrying would not change the outcome. She used her five senses to make sure that she was living in the present moment, rather than the negative imagined future in her mind, as much as possible. This helped her to manage her stress in a difficult situation.

Your Behavior

A final area of life over which you usually have at least some control is your own behavior. No matter what is going on in your life, you will usually have at least some choice about how you do or do not behave. If you dislike your job, you can choose to look for other work, or to seek some changes in your workplace. Of course, this may be easier said than done, and every situation is unique. But it is important not to dismiss the idea of trying to do something different. Prediction testing is a strategy that encourages behavior change. It requires you to try behaving in a way that is different from your usual behavior patterns and to find out what happens. We hope you have now had the chance to experience this method of taking control and the resulting positive impact on your stress.

Since behavior change is such a powerful stress reduction tool, the remaining chapters of this book focus on just that. These chapters discuss three key ways you can change your behavior in order to take control of stressful situations. The first one (assertiveness) involves changing the way you interact with others in order to stop you from taking on more than you can handle and can help you to get more of the things you want out of life. The second (time management) involves organizing your day and your life more efficiently. The final chapter (problem solving) helps you to generate solutions and action plans for practical problems in your life. Not everyone who feels stressed will need to make changes in all these areas. But before you say to yourself, "I manage my time efficiently" or "I already know how to solve problems—it's just that the problems in my life don't have solutions," give these lessons and exercises a try. You may be surprised at the results!

TASKS FOR STEP 7

There are no new tasks for this chapter. Continue to fill in your

- ✓ Daily Stress Record
- ✓ Progress Chart
- ✓ Prediction Testing Record
- ✓ Staying Present Record
- → When you feel confident with these techniques, continue on to Step 8.

STEP EIGHT

Be Assertive

Does this scene sound familiar? A friend or coworker asks you to do something that you really do not want to do, but you give in and agree to do it anyway. Then, later, another friend finds out and scolds you, saying, "Why in the world did you agree to that? You have got to be more assertive!" You now feel confused. Maybe you should have stood up for yourself; however, you did not want to seem pushy and selfish. You may not have asserted yourself because you thought it would cause stress, but it turns out that not asserting yourself is causing you stress, too.

Many people have a great deal of difficulty asserting themselves in a variety of situations. Some of these people are generally unassertive across almost all of life's settings, whereas others may simply have trouble asserting themselves in one or two situations. In either case, lacking assertiveness can often be the source of a great deal of stress in people's lives. This may be due to the worry and guilt they experience when they do try and assert themselves. Or it may be due to the anger and frustration they feel when they find themselves doing things that they just don't have time for and really should not be doing. Being more assertive therefore is an excellent way to make your environment less stressful (for example, doing less unnecessary work, getting help from people, and so on). We don't have space in this book to fully discuss all aspects of assertiveness training, but we will outline the key principles. If, at the end of this chapter, you feel that you need more help with assertiveness, you could check out one of several popular books on the market that cover the topic in detail or enroll in an assertiveness training course at a community health center, educational institution, or other public facility.

WHAT IS ASSERTIVENESS?

Before discussing how to be assertive, it is important that we clear up any misconceptions about assertiveness. Being assertive does not mean always getting your way. Rather, being assertive means developing a feel for your rights in a situation and feeling comfortable asking others to respect those rights. At the same time, you need to respect the rights of others and take those into account when deciding to act.

Psychologists distinguish between three types of behavior: unassertive, aggressive, and assertive. When you are unassertive, you let others always get their way, because you put their needs ahead of your own. When you are aggressive, you stomp over others because you see your needs as more important than the needs of others. But when you are assertive, you feel confident enough to express your own needs while at the same time acknowledging the needs of others. Some examples of the different types of expression are illustrated below.

Examples of Unassertive, Aggressive, and Assertive Behavior

Situation	Unassertive Response	Aggressive Response	Assertive Response
Being asked a favor that is not possible.	I guess I can try to fit it in.	You've got to be kidding.	I realize it is important to you, but I'm afraid my time is full up today.
Wanting to ask a favor that is not very pleasant.	Avoidance— meaning, don't ask.	I want you to do something for me.	It would really help me a great deal if you would do this for me.
Reacting to an inconvenience.	I guess I'll just live with it.	Stop that right now.	I would prefer if you could move elsewhere to do that.

The key to assertiveness is to insist on what you want only when it is appropriate. There are times when you really should insist on having your way, even if it causes some inconvenience to someone else. But there are other times when you have to put your own needs aside because the other person's needs are even more important. The trick is to learn the difference. Realistic thinking techniques can help in this process, as illustrated in the case studies below.

RHANI

Rhani had been repeatedly asked out on dates by Rod, a friend of her brother. Rhani had no interest in dating Rod. Although she made excuses whenever he asked her out, she told us that the situation was making her uncomfortable. We asked, "What would happen if you told Rod you did not want to go out with him?" Rhani replied that Rod would be hurt. But when she looked at that thought realistically, she realized that after all the times she had already said no, there was probably only a 50 percent chance that Rod would be hurt. Further, Rhani realized that she had been imagining a dire consequence of Rod's being hurt. She was assuming that he would never get over it. Even more, she believed that if Rod did not get over the rejection, it would be her fault.

Thinking realistically, Rhani saw that Rod probably would recover quite well if she asserted herself and told him she was not interested in dating him. And if he didn't recover, it would be Rod's responsibility, not hers. Rhani was not being nasty or cruel, but was realizing that she could not be expected to take responsibility for other people's feelings. In other words, if Rod took the chance of asking her out, he had to be prepared for her to say no, and Rhani could not be expected to do something she did not want to do just to keep Rod happy. If she did, the situation might never end. In other words, Rhani realized that she had a right to say no, and that in this case her right outweighed any consideration she might have for Rod's feelings. Importantly, however, Rhani had considered Rod's feelings and hadn't just blindly ignored them. When it came time for Rhani to be assertive, she was able to let Rod know that she had understood his feelings, but she was still able to clearly tell him that she didn't want to go out with him.

ERIK

Erik wanted to ask for a week off from work, only a month after he had taken a vacation, to make a final effort with his university work and finish his degree. Erik's initial thought was that his boss would say no. Realistically, however, he had to admit that he had no idea what his boss would say; therefore, the probability of a negative answer was only about 50 percent. So Erik asked himself, "What would happen if my boss did say no?" His fear, he realized, was that she would consider him lazy and fire him.

In fact, however, the evidence showed that Erik's boss had praised him in the past for his hard work. So even if she said no to the time off, she would be highly unlikely to fire him, or even to consider him lazy. Based on his realistic thinking, Erik realized that he should ask for the time off, since there was a chance he would get it, and whether he did or not, his boss would be unlikely to think badly of him or fire him. In addition, he felt that he had a right to ask for the time off since his university studies actually improved his capacity to do his work. In fact, in this case, Erik's boss did refuse his request but allowed him to take time off the following month. Because Erik had considered that his boss might say no (her right), he did not feel anger or resentment. At least he had a go, and he was going to have time off next month.

WHAT STOPS YOU FROM BEING ASSERTIVE?

There are two main reasons that people may not act assertively. First, many people just do not know the best words to use or know how to act in just the right way to get their point across.

These people may try to be assertive but may find themselves being misunderstood or taken advantage of, or they may come across as aggressive and threatening. Most people, however, do know how to be assertive. They just do not feel comfortable doing it, and they are never quite sure when it is the right thing to do. People in this second scenario often have others walk over them because they are worried that others may become angry at them or will not like them if they are assertive.

If you fall into the first category, then it will be useful to learn some strategies to help you get your way in a confident but non-threatening manner. We will discuss some simple strategies below. If you fall into the second group, then you need to treat your unassertiveness as a type of avoidance and then apply the techniques of realistic thinking, evaluating consequences, and prediction testing. By now these should be second nature to you, and we will simply describe some brief examples in this chapter.

ASSERTING YOURSELF

Learning to be assertive is fairly straightforward if you keep reminding yourself of the description of assertiveness we discussed above. Yet it is surprising how many people try to assert themselves in awkward ways. Many people either have difficulty getting their message across clearly or come across too strongly or aggressively. Do you remember the technique we learned earlier in the program: changing perspectives? This is a useful technique to employ here. When you want to be assertive with someone, try swapping places (mentally) with her and ask yourself, "If I were in her place, how would I respond to what I am about to say?" If your answer is, "I would feel angry" or "I would ignore it," then you are not expressing yourself well. Try some different ways of expressing yourself in your head and think about which one might have the best effect. Remember, if you make the other person angry, then she is going to become defensive and you will not get your way. The idea is not to score points or initiate combat, but to create a win-win situation in which you get what you want while at the same time the other person feels satisfied.

The most important thing is to use your common sense and think about how you are most likely to get your message across effectively. People are much more likely to listen if you are clear and confident in your expression and manner. They are more likely to help you if they understand your perspective and don't feel as though you are antagonistic toward them. Here are some simple rules to follow:

1. Watch your nonverbal actions.
Your message will be more likely to be heard and listened to if you give a confident and clear picture. Good eye contact, an upright, relaxed posture, and a clear voice give the image of someone who knows what he wants and is confident of getting it. When you look at the ground, shuffle your feet, or mumble, you give the impression that you are shifty or that you are not sure that you really want what you are asking for.

However, you also need to make sure that you don't come across as too overbearing. Make sure you don't stand too close, don't stare, and definitely keep your voice calm and level. Yelling only makes people defensive.

2. Be empathetic.

Remember, being assertive involves acknowledging that the other person in the situation also has rights and that they are important. When you make an assertive comment, you are much more likely to be listened to if you let the other person know that you recognize his or her side of the situation. For example, consider the following two statements: "I want you to stay back and finish this paperwork" and "I realize that you want to get home, but I need you to stay back and finish this paperwork." In the second statement, you are letting the person know that you realize that your request will cause an inconvenience. By acknowledging this, you are telling the person that her needs are of concern to you, but that you consider your needs more urgent at this time.

3. Use "I" statements.

"I" statements refer to talking about yourself when you say something, instead of talking in generalities. In other words, you should own your feelings. This is particularly important when you are expressing negative feelings. Consider the following two statements: "People have trouble breathing when you smoke in here" and "My breathing is irritated when you smoke in here." The first statement leaves you open to argument and resentment: "What do you know about people's breathing?" With the second statement, there is no possibility for argument, and it also gives the impression that you are being open and honest.

4. Describe the causes and effects.

Letting people know the entire situation, rather than simply making a demand, is much more likely to convince them that your rights and desires are important. In particular, when you want people to change something, it is useful to tell them exactly what it is that you want changed and why. For example, consider the following two demands: "Will you stop talking?" and "When you talk, it is hard for me to hear the film." The second version clearly indicates the behavior you are not happy with and its effect on you and is much more likely to be complied with and less likely to cause offense.

5. Suggest an alternative.

Following from the above rule, making a suggestion to people about alternative behavior that would be acceptable to you will further help to diffuse the situation. For example, something like the following would be good: "When you talk, it is hard for me to hear the film. Perhaps you could chat in the next room." By making a reasonable suggestion to people about how they could change, you are letting them know that you accept their right to do what they are doing. This strategy suggests that you are trying to find a mutually satisfactory solution.

DEALING WITH AGGRESSION

At times, no matter how careful you are with your assertiveness, you will find other people becoming aggressive toward you. This can be a source of intense stress. No one likes to be abused. Here are some suggestions for trying to minimize or combat aggression without becoming too stressed.

1. Don't buy in.

The main rule with aggression is not to buy into it and start being aggressive in return. When you are aggressive toward someone who is angry, it will only serve to increase their anger, and the whole interaction can spiral out of control. It is even better to back off and try again at a later time and place than to fuel the anger.

2. Keep calm.

The best way for you to diffuse someone's anger is to stay calm and in control. If you have a spare few seconds while the other person is being angry, try using your realistic thinking to help you control your own feelings. Is the other person really better than you? Is the other person really going to hit you? Is the other person going to get his or her way? Does it matter if the other person doesn't like you? And so on. Once you are able to calm your feelings, try to back this up with your manner. It is very hard for someone to get carried away with aggression if you are looking them confidently in the eye, speaking in a gentle, quiet manner, and standing in a relaxed, nonaggressive stance.

3. Use "I" statements.

As with the point above, it is much harder for someone to argue with you and get angrier if you own your own feelings and don't make broad sweeping statements.

4. Be empathetic.

Similarly, it is hard to be angry with someone who seems to understand your side of the story. Rather than just trying to force your view on the other person, try acknowledging his or her perspective. You are then much more likely to get your message across successfully.

5. Point out assumptions.

Sometimes people's anger is based on unstated assumptions or misunderstandings. Rather than simply hearing what the person is saying to you on a superficial level, try to step back a little mentally and see the situation from his side. Try to understand the underlying assumptions behind the person's anger. If you realize that there is a misunderstanding or that you are talking at cross purposes, you can then feed that back to the person in a calm and objective manner.

6. Stick to your point.

Finally, in some cases, it is just not possible to totally diffuse the situation. In these cases, it is often useful to repeat your message over and over. Each time, you should begin by acknowledging what the other person is saying, but then simply go on and repeat your message. For example, "I would like to see the manager, please," "Yes, I realize that it is very late, but I really do need to see the manager," "I know you would like to get home, but it is important for me to see the manager," and so on. Obviously, if the situation looks as though it might become violent, or you are really going to get nowhere, it is always better to back off and try again at a later time when everyone has calmed down.

WORRY ABOUT BEING ASSERTIVE

As we discussed above, possibly the main reason most people do not act assertively is not because they don't know how to express themselves, but because they worry about the effects of assertive behavior on others. In particular, they might worry that others will think they are pushy, aggressive, or demanding and that they will get angry or not like them. The stress management techniques that you have learned in earlier sections of this program will help you deal with these types of worries. In particular, you need to use realistic thinking and prediction testing to convince yourself that being assertive does not mean that other people won't like you or think you are pushy.

Realistic thinking, for example, can help you understand your reluctance to assert yourself. Clearly, a person who goes around demanding his or her own way all the time is not going to be too popular. But if you use assertiveness appropriately, after weighing the pros and cons in a given situation, people will respect you for standing up for your rights. Try asking yourself such realistic thinking questions as, "How likely is it that this person will be angry at me?" and "What is the worst that can happen if I ask?" The best form of evidence can often come by putting yourself in the other person's place, as we discussed in Step 4. For example, you could switch roles in your mind and ask yourself, "If this person were to ask the same favor of me, would I be angry?" In most cases, you will find that the answer is "no."

You might also want to look at your lack of assertiveness as a kind of avoidance and use prediction testing, as we discussed in Step 5. The first step is to identify the situations that you would normally avoid due to your negative predictions about being assertive. We have listed some common situations and examples below. Place a check next to the ones that apply to you:

Once you have identified the assertiveness situations that you avoid, it is time to start prediction testing. Use your Prediction Testing Record From to record your initial predictions, the evidence

	Situation	Example
☐	Saying "no"	Anne's brother often asked to borrow money. Anne always agreed, even though she couldn't really afford it.
☐	Asking for help	Anne needed help with a work project, but she didn't want to ask. So, she just worked late hours on her own, trying to get it done.
☐	Asking for change	Erik's neighbor often parked his car in Erik's parking space. Erik didn't say anything, even though it was very inconvenient.
☐	Delegating work	Erik's office had an assistant who was employed to assist the other staff with administrative tasks. But Erik didn't want to bother her so he did all his administration himself.
☐	Asking favors	Anne attended a weekly yoga class with her friend, Belle. Anne would have loved a ride home after class, but she felt embarrassed to ask.
☐	Changing your mind	Erik had bought a new coat, but upon getting it home decided that he didn't really like it. He felt uncomfortable about taking it back to the store, so he just kept it.

you will need to observe, and the outcome. Remember that you can do your assertiveness prediction testing slowly and gradually if you find it too stressful. Start with situations you find less challenging (such as asking your partner for a favor) and build up to those that are more challenging (like saying no to your boss). Don't forget to use your Prediction Testing Record Form for every assertiveness task that you do.

Assertiveness, like the other techniques you have tried, improves with practice. The more you act assertively, the easier it will become and you will find yourself having to deal with fewer unnecessary tasks or being loaded down less with work that you really shouldn't have to do.

We will end this lesson with Anne's case. You may remember that Anne had done some realistic thinking about asking her adult daughter, Ellie, to prepare the evening meals. This nervousness about asking others for help was a common feature in Anne's life, and greatly contributed to her stress. To address this problem, Anne worked out a list of assertiveness tasks to practice, which is shown here:

- ☐ Ask Ellie to help with the evening meals.
- ☐ Ask my friend Belle for a ride to yoga class.
- ☐ Ask a colleague for help on a work project.
- ☐ Ask my husband if he could take responsibility for grocery shopping from now on.
- ☐ Tell Tom I can't loan him money.
- ☐ Ask my boss to make some time to discuss my career goals.

Anne decided to start with the easier tasks, at the top of her list, and build up her confidence before attempting the harder ones at the bottom. For each task that she did, she practiced realistic thinking in her head. She then used her Prediction Testing Record to help test out her predictions. You can see part of her form here:

Event	Predictions—What Do I Expect to Happen?	Evidence to Look For—How Will I Know If My Predictions Come True?	Outcome—Did My Predictions Come True?
Ask Ellie for help with the evening meals.	She will be angry. She will say no.	Observe—What does she actually say? Does her body language and tone suggest anger?	No, she agreed to do it. She seemed a bit flat, but not angry.
Tell Tom that I can't loan him money.	He will be angry. He will think I'm selfish. He'll never speak to me again.	Observe—What does he actually say? Does his body language and tone suggest anger? If so, for how long does he stay angry?	Partly. He said that I had plenty of money, and that I was selfish. I practiced being assertive and held my ground. He stormed out, but later called and apologized.
Ask my boss to make time to discuss my career goals.	She will be too busy. She will seem irritated with me for wasting her time.	Observe—What does she actually say? Does her body language and tone suggest irritation?	No. She said that it was a great idea. She did say that she was busy this week, but we made a time next week. She smiled and sounded pleased—not irritated at all.

Anne found that practicing being assertive, and testing her predictions, reduced her stress considerably. She realized that most people in her life were reasonable and responded positively to her assertive requests. The exception was her brother Tom, who was known by all the family to have a bad temper. Anne accepted that she would always feel a little stressed about interacting with Tom because of his temper problems. What helped her here was her realistic thinking—she reminded herself that the temper was his problem, not hers. She also reminded herself that she was an adult and entitled to make her own decisions. She didn't need to agree with everything Tom said or wanted. Finally, Anne practiced keeping calm and repeating her message over and over, rather than becoming upset and backing down. This helped her to feel more confident and in control.

TASKS FOR STEP 8

✓ During the following week, try to pause before automatically agreeing to do things for other people. Once you break the habit of saying "yes" automatically, you can try telling people, "I'll think about whether I can do that for you, and get back to you." This is an interim step to learning to say "no" when you know immediately that you do not want to, or cannot, take on the additional responsibility.

✓ You may find that the people in your life are a little disappointed at first to find that they can no longer rely on you to agree to their demands. But you will also find that you resent them less for imposing on you, and you may want to reconsider relationships that seem based solely on your contributions—acquaintances who are never able to fulfill your requests but always expect you to help them out.

✓ Keep filling in your
  ✓ Daily Stress Record
  ✓ Progress Chart
  ✓ Prediction Testing Record
  ✓ Staying Present Record

Summary

- Lack of assertiveness is a major cause of stress for many people. In this lesson we looked at ways in which you could learn to be more assertive and save yourself a lot of stress in the long run.

- We discussed the definition of assertiveness and saw that being assertive means accepting both your own and the other person's rights.

- We looked at some strategies to help you get your message across better. These included:
  - Using clear and confident nonverbal actions.
  - Owning your own feelings.
  - Clearly spelling out the reasons for your feelings.
  - Coming up with possible alternatives.

- We also looked at ways of diffusing someone else's aggression.

- The main points were:
  - Keep and act calm.
  - Own your feelings.
  - Let the other person know that you can see their side of the issue.

- Finally, we looked at how you can use the techniques we learned earlier, especially realistic thinking and prediction testing, to help you become more comfortable with the idea of being assertive. Just like the other skills you have learned through this program, being assertive takes practice.

- Some people do not find asserting themselves difficult. If you are one of them, you can skip this assignment. But if assertiveness has been a problem for you, you should make a list of assertiveness situations for practice and prediction testing. You may not be able to plan opportunities to refuse other people's requests, but over the next week you should try to notice when you agree to do something. Ask yourself afterward if you really want to do, and have time for, whatever you agreed to do.

Manage Your Time

For many people, stress is either caused by or aggravated by time pressure, the feeling that there is too much to do in a day. To help you understand this pressure, consider our case study, Joe. Joe ran a real estate agency that employed 30 people. The company's business had been increasing rapidly, which made Joe happy but also caused him more stress. As the amount of work to be done grew, Joe took on more and more responsibility; he didn't trust anyone else to do it properly.

Soon, he had so many tasks to do that he did not know where to begin. Some days he spent far too much time doing unimportant things, and other times he simply stared out the window, too overwhelmed to choose one task and start it. Though he worked longer and longer hours, he never seemed to get enough done. His relationships with friends and family suffered, he lost sleep worrying about work, and eventually he developed an ulcer.

Most of us can identify to some extent with Joe's situation. It illustrates two typical problems associated with time pressure: taking on too much and working inefficiently. Taking on more responsibilities than you can handle does not mean you are a bad worker. In fact, you probably work so well that it seems natural to try to do more and more. This is when the second problem sets in. When you have more tasks than you can perform well, you feel overwhelmed, and your ability to work efficiently suffers. You need to learn to manage your time.

Some people have no problems at all with time pressure, and if this is true for you, you may find that this chapter is not that important. However, for others, time pressure is one of the most important sources of stress, and learning to manage time is one of the most important stress management techniques. Time management is no great mystery. It simply means learning to organize and allocate your time better so that you get the most out of your day without feeling stressed. Again, this comes back to an issue we discussed earlier, feeling that you have no control over your environment. By managing your time better, you are taking control of the world around you. As we will see later in this chapter, even if you cannot completely structure your time, it is important that you have some structure, or at least keep records and plans, so that you can achieve a sense of control.

The two main components of time management are designed to combat both problems described above. First, you will learn not to overcommit yourself. Next, you will learn to organize your time so that you complete your tasks efficiently and don't have to worry about forgetting things.

Which comes first, being overcommitted or being stressed? It's hard to say. People who tend to be stressed also tend to take on more than they can handle, and then, like Joe, they end up feeling even more stressed. Often this state of affairs sneaks up on you. It can be hard to say no to all the requests and opportunities that come along. We hope, by now, that you are practicing the assertiveness you learned in the previous chapter, so that saying no is becoming a little easier. But if you have not learned to be assertive, you may find that some of your overcommitment comes from being unassertive and taking on tasks that you really don't need to do.

Before you know it, the day is over, and you haven't even started the things you meant to do. As you have seen with the other stress management techniques, the first step is to become aware of what you are actually doing. To this end, you will be recording your activities for a few days so that you will have realistic evidence to act on. Before we continue, a word of warning: Time management takes time!

You may need to allow 15 to 30 minutes to record everything you do in a day. If you are already feeling overwhelmed, it may seem silly to take on another task; you will be tempted to ignore the reporting in favor of doing something else. But remind yourself that the recording is only temporary, and it will serve an important purpose. Though it takes time now, in the long run it will save you time by reducing your stress and helping you to work more efficiently. In other words, the time you save later will more than make up for the time you spend now.

RECORDING YOUR DAILY ACTIVITIES

Your first step is to record everything you do for the next few days. Try not to change your schedule to make it "look better." Simply record what you are actually doing on a few of your typically busy days. Recording for three or four days should be enough; the idea is simply to get a "sample" of your typical day. You should also try to record more than once a day so that you do not forget anything.

Recording at three or four regular intervals throughout the day should work well. We have prepared a **Daily Activity Record** for you to record your activities on page 100. If you have another record or planner that will accomplish the same thing, that's fine. Use the first column to write down everything you do, even things that were unplanned and fairly brief. In the second column, record the time that you started the task and the time that you stopped. Use those times to record the duration of the task in the third column, just so it will be easier to see how much time you spent. Finally, use the last column to record any comments on the task. Was it worth doing? Did you spend too long or not long enough? Were you interrupted often? Be sure to include things like sleep, personal care, time with spouse, and so on. The duration column should total to 24 hours. The record below shows part of such a form that was completed by Joe.

Joe's Daily Activity Record

Activity	Time	Duration	Comments
Work on next year's budget.	9:00	30min.	Wanted to spend longer.
Phone call.	9:30	10min.	
Question from Chloe re: sick employees.	9:40	5min.	She could have handled it.
Reading news online.	9:45	15min.	
Phone call.	10:00	5min.	
Phone call.	10:05	30min.	Could have tried to cut it off sooner.
Tidy filing cabinet.	10:35	35min.	Really Chloe's job.
Read about new accounting software.	11:10	35min.	More important things to do.
Work on next year's budget.	11:45	15min.	Too short—inefficient.
Lunch out with Hamish.	12:00	90min.	Fun but too long.

Once you have recorded your activities for three or four days, use the records to make four lists:

1. List the things you should have done or would have liked to do but didn't manage to get to during those days.
2. List the things you did not do properly because you did not have enough time.
3. List the things you should not really have been doing.
4. List the things that you spent too much time on.

The first two lists will help you decide whether you are overcommitting yourself. If there are many things in these lists that you should have done or didn't do properly, then you may be trying to fit too much into your day. If this is true, then it is no wonder you are stressed!

The next two lists will tell you if you are working inefficiently. If you find that much of your time is taken up by things that you should not really be doing or you are spending too much time on things, then your time is not being used as well as it could. Think of how much free time you would have to relax and enjoy life, if you rid yourself of some of these activities.

Here are the lists that Joe made:

Things I should have done/would like to do
Write ad for new employee.
Read Sally's report on production.
Go to get my hair cut.
Read Financial Review articles.
Talk to Steve about his review next week.

Things not done properly
Budget.

Things I shouldn't have been doing
Answering questions from Chloe that she could have handled.
Tidying filing cabinet.
Reading about accounting software.

Things taking too long
Lunch.
Phone call to property developer.

Deciding whether an activity has taken too long, or is not necessary, is very personal. Only you know what is efficient and what is not. The record of your daily activities should show you what you are doing each day so you are in a position to make such decisions. Sometimes it helps to get an outside perspective on your day by discussing the list with a friend or relative. The following case of Erik describes how the Daily Activity Record and priority lists can work.

ERIK

Erik had recently cut down from full time work to working four days per week. He had done this because he wanted to finally finish his architecture degree, which he had begun several years before. Erik had expected that having an extra day a week to work on his university work would reduce his stress significantly. Much to his dismay, however, he noticed that he felt just as busy and stressed as before.

In order to understand this better, Erik wrote down everything he did for three days, and he made lists of all the things he had not done or spent too much time on. When he studied these forms, he was surprised at what he saw. To begin, Erik noticed that it took him almost two hours to get out the door in the morning. He had been trying to walk for 30 minutes on the way to work each morning, but this rarely happened because he was usually running late. Erik realized that he spent much too long trying to locate different items in the morning—he would spend 10 minutes at a time trying to find his keys, searching for matching socks, trying to locate a clean shirt, and so on. He also noticed that he would become absorbed in the newspaper over breakfast, and sometimes spent half an hour reading when he should really be getting ready.

On his day off, Erik saw that he spent very little time actually writing his assignment as planned. Although he had done all the research he needed to the week before, Erik became worried that he didn't have enough references and spent an hour looking at additional resources online. He was persuaded by his brother to go with him to look at a new car, and this ended up taking much longer than anticipated. Then he found himself checking his work e-mail, even though he wasn't supposed to be at work that day, and getting distracted by some work issues. By the end of the day he had spent about two hours writing his assignment, rather than the six hours it would have taken to complete it.

Reading over your lists should lead you to some new realizations. How to act on those realizations is an individual decision. Some people like full days, when they are constantly on the go, while others need more "down time," to read, think, or just relax. If your lists are full of important tasks you have had to leave undone, then it's a pretty safe bet you are overcommitted. Even if your lists are short, you will probably notice ways in which you could use your time better.

Joe, for example, recognized two major problems with his workload after he had recorded his activities for three days. He found that he was wasting time on interruptions, which his personal assistant could easily screen and handle, such as phone calls and office questions. He also found that he was spending so much time on unimportant tasks that he did not have enough time for big projects. This is often true of people under stress. You keep doing the small things, the things you feel you can get done in a short time, but the big things that you are putting off begin to weigh more and more heavily upon you. Once you have recognized the problem, you can start doing something about it.

HOW TO GET MORE OUT OF YOUR DAY

Delegating

One of the most common discoveries that overcommitted people make is the large number of tasks they do in a day that could easily be done by someone else. This may happen for a number of reasons. It may be simply that you are too unassertive to ask others to do things for you. If this is the case, you need to go back to Step 8 and keep working on your assertiveness. However, it may be because you believe it is easier to do a task yourself than to explain it to someone else. Or perhaps you just do not think others will do the task as well as you would.

The only way out of this cycle is to ask other people to take on some of your responsibilities. If you can delegate only a couple of your regular tasks, you will be amazed at how much time it frees up. With more complicated tasks, like those at work, you may begrudge the time it takes to show someone else the ropes. But remember, the few minutes you invest in explaining now will save you time on every occasion in the future when that task needs doing. And if you find yourself worrying that the other person may not do the task as well as you do, remember your realistic thinking techniques. Ask yourself, "How likely is it that it won't be done properly?" And then ask, "What would really happen if the other person did it wrong?"

To return to the example of Joe, he realized that he should not be wasting his time answering phone calls from clients wanting to check on their properties. Knowing that his assistant was perfectly capable of handling the calls and passing along to him only the clients who had problems, he decided to ask his assistant to take over this responsibility. This, as it turned out, was easier said than done. When Joe analyzed his reluctance to delegate responsibility to his assistant, he realized that he was worried she would not give the clients accurate information. So he began challenging his thoughts. What was the probability that his assistant would give clients inaccurate information? Thinking realistically, Joe realized that his assistant knew the properties as well as he did, and it was highly unlikely that she would be wrong. But what if she was wrong? What would really happen if she made a mistake? After some thought, Joe realized that most of his clients would be understanding if she made a mistake—and, if any were not, he would be right there to step in. So by applying realistic thinking to time management, Joe was able to reduce his workload significantly.

Saying No

Many people run out of time because they spend so much of their day doing things they do not want to do—taking on the work of less efficient employees, for example, or talking to people who just will not go away. Being assertive is important in limiting how much you do in a day. By now, you should be working on your assertiveness skills. If saying no is a particular problem for you, make sure you include some practice of this skill into your prediction testing. Thinking realistically, you need to remind yourself that people will not be angry with you or hate you just because you do not have time to do something for them. If you can make yourself say no, even once or twice a day, you will find that you have a lot more time.

Our case study Erik realized that in order to make his day off work more productive, he needed to say no to any other invitations or requests on that day. Once he explained to his family the reason that he was taking the day off (to finish his university work) they were supportive of his decision to spend the whole day studying.

Sticking to Agendas

Another reason that some people run out of time is that they do a task in an inefficient way, or they start one task and end up doing several others. As an example of the first problem, let's say you have gotten into the habit of going out to lunch with a colleague every time you have an issue to discuss. If you want to go to lunch because it is fun or relaxing, that's fine. But if you are doing it simply to discuss business, then it may be far more efficient to write a memo or talk on the phone. Often, brainstorming ways in which you can make a task more efficient and thinking laterally about different ways of doing a task can help to get you out of many old and inefficient habits.

Erik, for example, decided to lay out his clothes for work the night before. He knew that he was not a "morning person" and generally took too long to find things in the morning. So, by getting organized the night before, he got out the door earlier and could get some exercise by walking to work.

Assessing Priorities

Perhaps the most important thing you must do once you realize you are overcommitted is to convince yourself that some things simply are not going to get done. You need to set priorities—in the short term, by deciding what to do each day, and in the long term, by deciding how you want to live your life.

For some people, giving up a task creates stresses all on its own. If this is true for you, go back to the realistic thinking strategies and use them to challenge your beliefs about giving up the task. Assessing priorities and organizing your time are so important that we will discuss them in more detail in the following section.

Labeling and Scheduling

Once you have examined your typical day, the next step is to assign each task a priority and work out a schedule so that the important things get done. It's easiest to start this by planning just one day—say, tomorrow. Make a list of all the things you plan to do tomorrow. Then go through the list and label the tasks according to how important they are. It is best to assign importance in terms of four levels: A, B, C, and D tasks.

- A tasks are top priority. Give an A only to tasks that absolutely, positively have to be done that day. Some days you may have no A tasks, while other days you may have several. Be strict with the label. Ask yourself, "Do I really have to do this today?" If not, it is not an A task. If you have too many A tasks, then you are probably overcommitting yourself.
- B tasks are the most common type—things that are important but do not necessarily have to be done immediately. Of course, if they are not done, B tasks will eventually become A tasks. You should not feel stressed if you cannot get to a B task immediately because you know that it is not the top priority. There is always tomorrow. But do try to do it before it becomes an A task, to keep stress at a minimum.

- C tasks are those that will need to be done someday, but at the moment they are not too important. Some C tasks can stay C tasks indefinitely, while others will eventually become B or even A tasks. C tasks are useful to fill in the gaps in your day. That way, if you are running behind schedule, you can always cancel a C task to give you more time without getting too stressed.
- D tasks are all those tasks that can be delegated to someone else. Most of the time, these tasks will come from the other priority tasks on your agenda. In other words, you might first assign a task a B priority. Then, when you look at it more closely, you realize that you can actually hand the task (or part of the task) to someone else, making it into a D task. Obviously, the more tasks you can turn into D tasks, the easier your day.

Once you have divided up your tasks this way, the next step is to organize them. Use a recording sheet like the **Daily Planner** on page 101. Many electronic diaries or software programs also have good ways to arrange your day.

The first step is to look over your list of A, B, and C tasks and see how many can actually be allocated to D priority. Next, write on the sheet all the tasks that must be done at a specific time, such as attending a meeting, picking up your children, or having lunch with a client. Then, beginning with the A tasks, write the other tasks into time slots when you think you can do them. Do not schedule all the A tasks together. Instead, follow an A task with a B or C task. That way, if something keeps you from doing the A task or it takes longer than expected, you can reschedule the B or C task and still get the A task done.

JOE'S SAMPLE DAILY PLANNER

Time Task Rating (A, B, C, D)
8:00–9:00 Reply to e-mails: A
8:15–9:00 Work on next month's advertising campaign: B
9:00–10:00 Meet with accountant: A
10:00–11:00 Work on advertising campaign: B
11:00–12:00 Staff meeting: B
12:00–12:30 Lunch: C
12:30–1:30 Meet with Mike to discuss his new role: A
1:30–2:00 Practice relaxation: C
2:00–3:00 E-mails: B
2:30–4:00 Go through last month's performance figures for sales reps: B
4:00–5:00 Work on plans for rearranging office space: B
5:00–5:40 Read *Financial Review* articles: C
6:00–7:00 Tennis: C

FLEXIBILITY AND REWARDS

Joe's daily plan illustrates two important factors you should consider in making your own: staying flexible and "rewarding" yourself. Making a daily plan is supposed to reduce your stress, not increase it. If you schedule your tasks so tightly that any interruption throws the whole schedule off, then you may not be able to stick to the schedule and you are likely to feel even more stressed. If you put all of the unpleasant tasks together, both your efficiency and your mood may soon suffer.

When you are scheduling your tasks, especially the most important ones, estimate realistically how long the task will take and then at least double that time. Tasks almost always take longer than you expect. You are bound to run into unexpected hitches, interruptions, or emergencies that distract you. So give yourself plenty of time.

You will be surprised at how much you can get done in a day when you organize it logically, even if you allow a lot of time for each task. And wouldn't you agree that it is better to end your day with three completed tasks than six half-finished ones?

Approach the scheduling realistically; plan for how your day really goes, not how you wish it would go. That means allowing for any time-consuming events that are likely to happen, whether you like them or not.

It is also important to schedule rewards—in other words, to schedule rests or enjoyable tasks after particularly difficult jobs. This practice gives you a break, helps you to relax, and helps to make you more efficient as you move on to the next task. Often, C tasks are more fun than A or B tasks and you can use them as rewards, as Joe did. You will notice that Joe scheduled a pleasant C task at the end of his day (reading). This helped him to unwind after a long day and also allowed him the flexibility to have more time for his earlier A and B tasks if these had not been finished. A different type of reward is to look over your planning sheet at the end of the day and check off all the tasks you completed. Chances are, you will end up with a strong feeling of accomplishment.

What do you do with any tasks that have not been completed? We hope these will not be A tasks, but will be B and C tasks. Because they are not essential tasks for today, putting them off until tomorrow should not cause too much stress. You should think about whether these tasks need to have their priorities reassigned (for example, will any of today's B tasks become tomorrow's A tasks?). Then you should simply make a note of them in order to schedule them into tomorrow's plan. This will let you finish your day with a feeling of being in control of your time.

If you find that you are finishing most of your days with a lot of unfinished tasks, then this is a clear message that you are not being realistic in your daily planning. You need to be more generous in the time you allow for tasks, and you need to try and fit less into a day. If unexpected interruptions keep interfering with your plans, then you need to schedule into your day enough time to cover those interruptions. That way, the interruptions, in a sense, become planned activities, and you will feel more in control.

A WORD ABOUT PROCRASTINATION

Often when we have one really major job to do, we try and find every excuse under the sun to try and avoid it. Suddenly, all sorts of minimal tasks become high priority. The major task then becomes more and more urgent and stress levels increase. If this describes you, then you need to do something about your procrastination in order to reduce your stress.

The first thing to do is to try and determine why it is that you are procrastinating. There are three main reasons. First, you may just not like doing the particular task and you may be letting the negative feelings about it build up and up. There is not much that you can do about this, except to use some motivational strategies. Set yourself some specific goals (for example, two hours' work on the task each day). Then tell a friend, colleague, or relative about your goals and arrange a time to review your progress with them. Their expectations will motivate you to stick to your commitment. You may also need to remind yourself that we all come across tasks that are unpleasant, and sometimes we just have to put up with some unpleasantness in our lives. Finally, reward yourself for meeting your goals. Sometimes the sense of achievement will be reward enough, but consider also rewarding yourself with an enjoyable activity for particularly difficult tasks.

Another reason for procrastinating is because of anxiety or stress about the finished product. Some people worry so much about getting things perfect, or they worry so much about not being able to do something well enough, that they don't do it at all. Obviously, this is unrealistic—surely it is better to do something reasonably than not at all. If you find yourself thinking in this way, you need to apply the techniques you learned in the earlier steps of this program to your procrastination. In particular, the realistic thinking techniques will be important. Look at how likely it is that you will do a bad job, and if you do, so what? Then, apply prediction testing to the task. Break the task down into small steps, put them in order of difficulty (in most tasks you will find some sections that are easier than others), and then force yourself to do them, one step at a time, looking for evidence of your predictions. Often, telling yourself that your boss (or whoever) doesn't have to see the first draft is a way of taking some of the pressure off so that you can at least get started. If you find that this is a general problem in your life—in other words, if you are generally perfectionistic—then you need to treat your perfectionism as an area for prediction testing. You need to develop a list consisting of different tasks that involve making mistakes, letting other people down, and so on and work out your negative predictions. Then you need to do each of these tasks in order of difficulty and look for evidence for your predictions. Finally, you can use this evidence in your realistic thinking. Ultimately, you need to learn that not doing something perfectly does not mean you are a failure.

Finally, many people simply do not know how to go about beginning a task, and the more they think about it, and the longer they leave it, the more overwhelming it seems. The best way to attack this type of problem is to break the larger task into many small sections. Rather than just trying to begin, sit down and write out an overall plan. In this plan, make sure you point out all of the sections and subsections to the task. Then, you should pick one section and ignore the others—pretend they don't even exist—and simply work on that one section. Once you have finished a rough draft of that first section, go on to the next and so on. At each point, you need to intentionally make yourself forget about the fact that this is part of a larger, overall project. Try to think of it as a number of small projects and focus on the present as you do each one. Using your time management principles and planning out your days will help you to get through all of the sections.

TASKS FOR STEP 9

Your assignment for this week is for three or four days to record your daily activities using the Daily Activity Record and make your priority list indicating the other things you want to get done.

- ✓ For the remainder of the week begin to organize your time by using your Daily Planner.
- ✓ Keep filling in your
    - ✓ Daily Stress Record
    - ✓ Progress Chart
    - ✓ Reality Testing Record

Summary

In this lesson we have shown you the importance of managing your time.

- Taking on too many tasks and performing them inefficiently can be a leading cause of stress for many people. Even if you believe that you manage your time efficiently, you should follow our suggestions in this lesson; you will be amazed at what you discover.
- You now have some tips on how to reduce your daily stress level by:
    - Not overcommitting.
    - Delegating.
    - Saying no.
    - Sticking to an agenda.
    - Prioritizing.
- Labeling your tasks on a scale of A through D can not only help you prioritize your tasks, it can also add to your self-esteem when you see how much you "really" do accomplish.

Daily Activity Record

Activity	Time	Duration	Comments
_____	_____	_____	_____
_____	_____	_____	_____
_____	_____	_____	_____
_____	_____	_____	_____
_____	_____	_____	_____
_____	_____	_____	_____
_____	_____	_____	_____
_____	_____	_____	_____
_____	_____	_____	_____
_____	_____	_____	_____
_____	_____	_____	_____
_____	_____	_____	_____
_____	_____	_____	_____
_____	_____	_____	_____
_____	_____	_____	_____
_____	_____	_____	_____
_____	_____	_____	_____
_____	_____	_____	_____
_____	_____	_____	_____
_____	_____	_____	_____

Daily Planner

Time	Task	Rating (A, B, C, D)	✓ Done
_____	_____	_____	_____
_____	_____	_____	_____
_____	_____	_____	_____
_____	_____	_____	_____
_____	_____	_____	_____
_____	_____	_____	_____
_____	_____	_____	_____
_____	_____	_____	_____
_____	_____	_____	_____
_____	_____	_____	_____
_____	_____	_____	_____
_____	_____	_____	_____
_____	_____	_____	_____
_____	_____	_____	_____
_____	_____	_____	_____
_____	_____	_____	_____
_____	_____	_____	_____
_____	_____	_____	_____
_____	_____	_____	_____
_____	_____	_____	_____

Solve Problems

Sometimes stress is caused by exaggerated worries that lend themselves well to realistic thinking and prediction testing. But sometimes you have problems that are not exaggerated; they are difficult, and you really cannot think of a solution. Problems like these, for which the right course of action is not always clear, can greatly increase your stress. You may find yourself lying awake at night thinking about these problems, or having trouble concentrating at work because of all the issues on your mind.

You need a way to deal with these problems. The following technique should help when you have trouble thinking of a solution to a problem. The technique is very simple and makes common sense. It is also effective.

Basically, it is an extension of realistic thinking, which you are already good at. The technique addresses the two things that happen when you face a difficult problem: you feel too overwhelmed to define the problem clearly, and you feel that no possible solution exists. Let's look at these two issues separately.

DEFINING THE EXACT PROBLEM

It is difficult to believe at first, but even when you are feeling so overwhelmed by a problem that you seem to think about nothing else, you may not be seeing the problem clearly. People tend to think of their problems in very broad, vague ways that assume the worst. So your first task will be to think through the specific, objective details of the problem. In other words, ask yourself, "What exactly is the problem here?" As usual, writing out your thoughts can help you organize them.

The **Problem Solving Record** on page 109 may be helpful to you in writing out your thoughts. In the first column, write exactly what the problem is. This may take some thought. You want specific details, not vague descriptions. And you want the actual, objective problem, not your feelings about it.

Let's say, for example, that you are having trouble with employees who are not showing up regularly for work. You could write, "Employees not showing up for work," but that is vague. You could write, "Stupid employees care nothing about their jobs," but that, obviously, is a bit emotional! It is also catastrophizing, or assuming the worst possible motive. Instead, a good practical description of the problem might read like this: "Two employees (Mark and Jan) did not come in to work two days this week."

Problems are not always what they seem on the surface. But you cannot solve them until you find out what they really are. In other words, you must find the cause or root of the problem. For example, if your child is not doing well in school, there could be any number of solutions, depending on what is causing the problem. In this case, defining the problem as "My son is not doing well at school" would not be nearly as useful as stating, "My son's school is not teaching properly" or "My son is not interested in schoolwork."

Defining the problem specifically is critical in helping you find a solution. Take some time to think about what is really at the root of the problem. Sometimes you can think and think and still not know the cause of a problem. Then that becomes your problem, and you can apply the problem-solving technique to this issue first. In other words, in the problem column you could write, "Not knowing why my son is doing poorly at school." When you move on to the next step of the technique, coming up with solutions, all your solutions will be aimed at trying to find out why your son is not doing well. Once you know that, you can work on a solution to that problem.

BRAINSTORMING

Just as people often have trouble defining a problem, they also have trouble believing that any solution to the problem exists. But in fact, nearly every problem has a solution; sometimes it is just hard to think of it. This is when you can try "brainstorming." Brainstorming means letting your mind go and writing down every possible solution to the problem, no matter how impractical or ridiculous it sounds. The idea is simply to get your mind working. When you do, you may happen upon a solution that never would have occurred to you otherwise. Therefore, anything you think of, no matter how dumb it sounds, can help by leading you to another possibility.

Let's say, for example, that your problem is that your neighbor's dog is keeping you awake at night by barking. After writing that problem in the first column of the form, you proceed to the second column and brainstorm these ideas: talking to your neighbors, asking them to sell the dog, asking them to keep the dog inside at night, and poisoning the dog. We hope you would not seriously consider poisoning the dog! But writing down this idea helps you vent your frustrations and may lead you to another idea, such as calling the police. Once you have written down every possible solution you can think of, decide which ones are practical (poisoning the dog may be possible, but it certainly is not responsible!). Then rank them.

As a second example, think of the situation we discussed before in which your two employees did not turn up to work on two days. Obviously the first step here is to find out why. Let's say that you found out that there is no legitimate reason, and so you are wondering about their commitment. You might then brainstorm the following possible solutions: explain to them the importance of being on time, let it go, beat them up, fire them, or give them a last chance with a clear ultimatum. Clearly, when you look over this list, you would decide that the third solution is not practical, and you might also decide that the second one is not helpful for your business. So, this leaves you with three possibilities.

DEVISING A PLAN OF ACTION

The last step is to consider each possible solution and to decide which is most likely to give you the answer you want. In many cases, there could be more than one way to solve your problem. In this case, you need to think through the pros and cons of each alternative and then rank order the possible solutions from the best to worst. Sometimes it is useful to use your realistic thinking skills to help rank the solutions. For example, you could ask yourself, "How likely is this solution to work?" and "If it does not work, what could the consequences be?"

For example, your problem may be that your car is having mechanical trouble. One solution would be to buy a new car. The probability that this solution would work is 100 percent. The consequences would include the high cost, the great amount of time it would take, and so on. Another solution would be to have the car repaired. The probability that this solution would work may be only 80 percent. But the consequences might include this solution being less expensive and relatively quick. Listing probabilities and consequences can make it easier for you to decide which solution you prefer to try first.

Returning to our employee example, you may decide that simply talking to your employees has the least unpleasant consequences, but is also the least likely to work. On the other hand, firing your employees would have the worst consequences (you would lose two employees who know the business and you would have to go through the hassle of advertising for their replacements, recruiting, and so on). Therefore, you may decide that the option of giving them an ultimatum is the best for everyone, and this would be your first choice. However, you might then keep the firing option as your second choice if the first one does not work.

The list in the last column now becomes your plan of action. First, you will try the solution that seems best. If that does not work, or cannot be accomplished for some reason, you can move on to the next solution on the list. You should also continue to apply your realistic thinking techniques to the problem, even after you have listed the potential solutions. Sometimes when you ask yourself, "What is the worst that can happen if this problem is not resolved?" you will be surprised at how nonthreatening the answer is. Here are two cases to illustrate the technique.

ERIK

Erik's doctor had told him many times that he needed to lose weight. Although he had been aware of this problem for some time, Erik had never managed to arrive at a solution. He had started thinking of himself as "undisciplined" and "lazy." These thoughts made him feel unhappy and therefore even less capable of tackling the problem.

Rather than engaging with these judgmental and unhelpful explanations, we encouraged Erik to try some structured problem solving. His first task was to define the problem, which he stated as, "I'm fat." This was a very general and subjective description, so we encouraged him to be more specific. Erik then stated, "I am 25 pounds over my healthiest weight." We then asked Erik about his understanding of the problem. Had his doctor discussed with him some of the causes of excess weight gain? Yes, she had. Erik understood that the most likely reasons for his current weight were his frequent consumption of high-calorie take-out food, and his lack of regular exercise. We suggested that he approach each of these causes as separate problems, and to choose one to work on first. Erik chose exercise, and thus came to his final, and most exact, description of the problem: "I don't have a realistic exercise routine."

The next step was for Erik to brainstorm a list of possible solutions. We encouraged him to keep an open mind and to write down all the ideas he thought of, regardless of whether they seemed

Erik's Problem Solving Record

Define the Problem	Possible Solutions	Pros and Cons	Plan of Action
First attempt: I'm fat.	Join a gym.	Expensive. Have done this before and didn't go.	1. Get off the bus early and walk for 30 minutes to get to work each day.
Can you be more specific?	Walk to work.	Too far, but could get bus part of the way.	2. Call Jess and ask if we can walk on the weekends instead of going out for coffee.
I am 25 pounds overweight.	Get a personal trainer.	Would be motivating but too expensive.	
Do you know the root or cause of the problem?	Join a soccer team.	Might be fun, but am not fit enough yet.	3. Make appointment with doctor to get her ideas.
Eating high-calorie foods.	Jog in the morning before work.	Cheap, but hard. Don't think I'm motivated enough.	
Not exercising.	Do a long walk with a friend on weekends.	Enjoyable but can only be done on weekends.	
Exact problem: I don't have a realistic exercise routine.	Ask my doctor for help in planning a routine.	Would keep me accountable. Don't want to take up her time.	

workable or not. With this approach, Erik was able to write down several possible solutions, including joining a gym, getting a personal trainer, walking to work, joining a soccer team, walking with a friend on the weekends, jogging in the mornings, and asking his doctor for suggestions. Erik then reviewed these options in turn and considered the pros and cons of each one.

Finally, Erik designed an action plan comprising his most practical solutions. Although he acknowledged that the problem would take time to resolve, Erik reported feeling much more positive and in control. Taking a structured problem solving approach allowed Erik to see solutions to a problem that he had previously dismissed as too difficult to address.

ANNE

Anne and her family had been under financial strain since her husband was laid off from his job the year before. Although they had managed by cutting down expenses, Anne was now dismayed to learn that their car needed expensive repairs. Normally, a discovery like this would cause Anne many sleepless nights of worry. This time, however, Anne decided to take a problem solving approach and face her worries head-on. You can see Anne's problem solving record below.

Anne's Problem Solving Record

Define the Problem	Possible Solutions	Pros and Cons	Plan of Action
First attempt: We're broke.	Sell the car.	Would get money quickly. But we may be able to get it fixed when Jon gets another job.	1. Get bus and train timetables. Use public transport until we can afford the car repairs.
Can you be more specific? We don't have enough money to pay for car repairs.	Keep the car but don't use it until we can afford to have it repaired.	Won't cost money. But will have to think about other forms of transport.	2. Speak to Ellie and Jon about having a garage sale.
Do you know the root or cause of the problem?	Try to get another credit card and put the charge on that.	High interest rates. The stress of more debt.	3. Be supportive of Jon while he looks for work.
Jon losing his job.	Have a garage sale and try to raise some money by selling things we don't need.	Hard work. Could make some money. Would de-clutter the house.	
Exact problem: We won't have enough money to pay for car repairs until Jon gets another job.	Pressure Jon to look harder for a job.	Could strain our relationship. He is looking pretty hard already.	
	Take money from petty cash at work.	Illegal and wrong. I would feel even more stressed!	

Anne was surprised to notice how much better she felt after sitting down and completing this process. Normally, her worries seemed to cycle around and around, without ever reaching a clear solution. This time, however, Anne was able to come up with a plan that seemed both practical and effective. She still longed for the day that her family would have a better income, but her stress level was significantly reduced.

TASKS FOR STEP 10

✓ Try this technique with a problem that has been bothering you lately using the Problem Solving Record. Follow all four steps:
  ✓ Identify the problem—be specific and consider the root or cause.
  ✓ Brainstorm solutions.
  ✓ Consider the pros and cons.
  ✓ Plan action.
✓ Try out the first solution on your list, and evaluate the results. If you are not satisfied, go on to the next solution.
✓ No pressing problems this week? You may still want to practice this technique, either by using your imagination and inventing a problem, by following one of the examples in this chapter, or by applying problem solving to an issue you resolved successfully in the past. Considering other solutions to a problem you have already solved can help you increase your flexibility for the future.
✓ Keep filling in your
  ✓ Daily Stress Record
  ✓ Progress Chart
  ✓ Daily Planner
  ✓ Prediction Testing Record

Summary

- Changing your environment to reduce your stress often involves finding solutions to very real and difficult problems. In this step we discovered that the first step to solving these problems is to identify the exact problem.
- Once a problem has been clearly identified, brainstorming possible solutions can help to identify answers that are logical and practical.
- Listing the possible solutions, in their order of priority, can then lead to a plan of action for solving the problem.

Problem Solving Record

Define the Problem	Possible Solutions	Pros and Cons	Plan of Action

First attempt:

_____   _____   _____   _____

_____   _____   _____   _____

_____   _____   _____   _____

Can you be more
specific?

_____   _____   _____   _____

_____   _____   _____   _____

_____   _____   _____   _____

Do you know the root
or cause of the problem?

_____   _____   _____   _____

_____   _____   _____   _____

_____   _____   _____   _____

Exact Problem:

_____   _____   _____   _____

_____   _____   _____   _____

_____   _____   _____   _____

CONCLUSION

Kick off your shoes, relax, and think about where you were before you started this program. Did stress seem like a big mystery, an ugly dragon you had to battle every day to stay in control of your life? Now think about your situation today, after months of practicing stress management techniques. Are you feeling calmer and more in control? When you feel the symptoms of stress coming on, do you find yourself thinking, "OK, I know what this is, and I know what to do about it"? Great, give yourself some credit! None of us feel calm every day of our lives, but you have come a long way from the person who filled out those first forms. If you don't believe that, just look back at the forms and you will see. It is important to keep your expectations realistic—after all, you don't want the process of mastering stress to cause you more stress! You cannot expect every one of your records to show zero stress.

As we have emphasized throughout the book, having some stress in your life is not only natural but healthy. It helps keep you motivated, and it keeps your life challenging enough to be interesting. You should also remember that the skills you have been learning are designed to last a lifetime. They will never be perfect, but they will become more effective the more you practice them. By now, for example, you can probably do your relaxation at will, wherever you happen to be. Just think how different that is from the first time you sat with your eyes closed in a dark room, struggling to concentrate.

As we have repeated throughout this book, the problem is not that you experience stress; the goal of this program is not to make you an unresponsive zombie. The problem is that you previously experienced stress so intensely or excessively that it controlled and ruined your life. We hope stress now no longer runs your life, and your feelings of anxiety, anger, frustration, and so on are within manageable levels.

Before we send you out to a lifetime of practice, we need to make one last point. No matter how skilled you become at practicing your relaxation techniques, there will probably be times in your life when circumstances leave you feeling extremely stressed. Everyone faces major upheavals—a loved one dying, a business failing, a family crisis coming to a head. When you face such situations, remind yourself of two very important things. First, feeling stress in trying times is natural and expected; there is a perfectly rational explanation for your response, and it's part of being human—everyone's life is punctuated with crises. But these things pass, and no matter how bad you feel, remember too that you are better off than you would have been before, because now you possess specific skills to help keep your stress from becoming excessive or going on longer than it should.

When you come up against a major life event that leaves you feeling highly stressed again, you need to remind yourself that you now have the skills to quickly regain control. Don't be embarrassed to go back to basics and work through the skills in this program again. This is not an admission of defeat. You just have to remind yourself that, for all of us, sometimes life gets on top of us. When this happens, going back to your basic practice should quickly remind you of the skills you have learned. It will not take as long to master your stress the second time as it did this time.

Remember the basic message throughout our program. The more you practice, the more success you will have. If you incorporate realistic thinking and the other exercises into your daily life, they will become so automatic that you will not even notice you are doing them. You will just notice the effect—a calmer you. With your stress under control, you should be able to get excited about things again, and actually enjoy your job, your family, and your friends.

STOPPING MEDICATION USE

If you were taking a prescription drug for stress before you started this program, you may now be ready to stop taking it—if that's what you want to do. We have not addressed this topic before now because it was important for you to learn to master your stress before stopping your medication. About half the people who were taking medication for stress feel ready to stop taking it by the time they finish this program. Many others stop within a year.

But do not rush yourself; there is no need to stop your medication until you are ready. And remember that you should *always* work with your doctor when making any change involving prescription medication.

Common Medication for Stress

The medications most commonly prescribed for relief of short-term stress are minor tranquilizers, most of which are part of a class known as benzodiazepines. This group includes dozens of types and brand names, among them clonazepam (Klonopin), diazepam (Valium), and alprazolam (Xanax).

These medications usually are prescribed only for short periods because people develop a tolerance for them. In other words, after a few weeks you would need more and more of the benzodiazepine to produce the same effect, and you would run the risk of becoming dependent on it.

If you did develop dependence, you would experience withdrawal symptoms when you stopped taking it. For this reason, most doctors prescribe these minor tranquilizers only to help a patient through a difficult situation, not for long-term use.

Antidepressants are prescribed for long-term stress and anxiety. The most commonly prescribed are a category called selective serotonin reuptake inhibitors (SSRIs), which include sertraline (Zoloft), escitalopram (Lexapro), paroxetine (Paxil), fluoxetine (Prozac), and fluvoxamine (Luvox). Other categories include serotonin and noradrenaline reuptake inhibitors (SNRIs) such as venlafaxine (Effexor) and reversible inhibitors of monoamine oxidase A (RIMAs) such as moclobemide (Aurorix). Antidepressants can be taken for a longer time and are easier to withdraw from than the minor tranquilizers.

If you wish to stop using medication, we strongly encourage you to follow these guidelines and listen to your prescribing doctor:

- Withdraw slowly. Despite what you may have seen in the movies, "cold turkey" is not the way to go. Ask your doctor to help you work out a schedule for diminishing your dosage gradually.
- Set a target date. You and your doctor should pick a date by which you hope to be completely off medication. This date should be far enough away to allow for gradual tapering off, but not so far away that your goal seems unreachable.
- Use your stress management techniques.

Eliminating your medication is nothing to get stressed about! Most people can cope quite well with a gradual decrease in dosage. But some people find that their feelings of stress temporarily grow stronger as they begin withdrawing from a medication. This kind of "outbreak" of stress nearly always goes away after a week or two, as the medication clears out of your system. If you experience an outbreak, simply do your relaxation and try the other techniques you have been using all along. You may have to put up with a little discomfort as your body adjusts to the change in order to give up your medication.

For example, you may think that you are having a total relapse or that your anxious feelings will never end. But how likely is that, really? You just learned that a lot of people feel this way for a few days when they stop taking their tranquilizers, and that it does go away. Also, if you have been taking a small amount of a medication for a long time, your body may have little or no reaction, but you may feel insecure about not having your pills with you. Some of our clients carry pill bottles with them for a long time without ever taking a pill. (Some people even get the same secure feeling carrying an empty bottle.)

In this case, the stressful situation you are facing is being without pills. But what do you think would happen if you went a day or two without carrying your pill bottles around? Whatever that is, how likely is it to happen? And would it be so terrible if it did? Try some prediction testing on this situation. Go for a day without carrying your pill bottle—then two days. Check out what really happens—you might be surprised by the result. Utilizing your relaxation and realistic thinking, along with other stress reduction procedures, can help you stop taking medication for stress.

In a few people, withdrawal from a benzodiazepine can cause severe anxiety or panic attacks. Your doctor can help adjust your schedule to cope with this problem. Additionally, there are some very good nonmedication programs around for the treatment of panic attacks.

For further reading on this topic, the following book is recommended: M. W. Otto & M. H. Pollack (2009). *Stopping Anxiety Medication Workbook*, Second Edition. New York: Oxford University Press.

CONGRATULATIONS

We hope that you enjoyed using this stress management program and that you got a lot out of it. By now your stress is hopefully much more under control. But remember that it is never a problem to go back and remind yourself of some of the lessons or to even start the program again. Although you shouldn't need to practice all of the techniques formally or for long periods every day now, it is still important to practice regularly and to build all of the strategies into your daily life. In this way you will be able to keep mastering your stress for the rest of your life.

ABOUT THE AUTHORS

David H. Barlow, PhD, is Professor of Psychology and Psychiatry and Founder and Director Emeritus of the Center for Anxiety and Related Disorders at Boston University. He received his PhD from the University of Vermont in 1969 and has published more than 500 articles and chapters and more than 60 books, mostly in the area of the nature and treatment of emotional disorders. He is the recipient of numerous awards, including the Distinguished Scientific Award for Applications of Psychology from the American Psychological Association and the James McKeen Cattell Fellow Award from the Association for Psychological Science, which honors individuals for their lifetime of significant intellectual achievements in applied psychological research.

Ronald M. Rapee, PhD, is Distinguished Professor of Psychology at Macquarie University in Sydney, Australia, and Director of the Centre for Emotional Health. Professor Rapee's primary research focuses on the understanding and management of anxiety and related disorders across the lifespan. He has established a number of internationally used treatment programs and was recently awarded the Order of Australia for his contributions to clinical psychology.

Sarah Perini, MA, is Director of the Emotional Health Clinic at Macquarie University in Sydney, Australia, where she teaches postgraduate psychology students how to conduct effective treatment. She is an experienced clinical psychologist who has treated hundreds of stressed and anxious patients. She has also worked in a range of clinics and hospitals and has published several academic articles.